IF I CAN'T BE THE CAKE, I WON'T BE THE CRUMZ
The Cake Chronicles for a Healthy, Long Lasting Relationship

Copyright © 2017 by Delbra Brown
All rights reserved.

Cake Chronicles is a trademark of D.A. Brown Consulting dba Hoosevents LLC
If I Can't Be The Cake, I Won't Be The Crumz is a trademark of D.A. Brown Consulting dba Hoosevents, LLC

All rights reserved. No part of this book may be reproduced in any form or by any means electronic or mechanical, without prior written consent of the publisher except for the inclusion of brief quotes in a review.

Printed in the United States of America
Version II - 11/2017

ISBN-10:0-9990738-0-X
ISBN-13:978-0-9990738-0-3

Published by D.A. Brown Consulting dba Hoosevents, LLC
www.DABrownConsulting.com

DISCLAIMER: The purpose of this workbook is to help those who desire to develop loving, healthy, relationships with others. This book should be used as an educational tool and while the concepts identified in this book are based on psychological and coaching theories, no therapeutic benefits are offered or implied. Therapy and coaching sessions are a process that is offered between the professional and their client, the tools identified in this book can help individuals identify areas in their life they may need to re-evaluate and if the individual is not able to identify solutions by walking through this self-healing process, consult a therapist or a professional life/relationship coach who can help you work through some of the behavior issues identified. The reader should consult proper medial advice in matters relating to his/her mental health and particularly with respect to any symptoms that may require diagnosis or mental health attention.

Cover Design and Cake Chronicles Graphics designed by Jason Harvey

Cake Chronicles Coaching 80/20 Life/Relationship services provided by
Delbra Brown
Rochester NY 14606
(585) 317-4313
info@CakeChronicles.com
info@DABrownConsulting.com

Discount pricing offered to educational and organizational institutions that desire to use this self-help guide in volume or a group setting. Contact Mrs. Brown for details on volume pricing.

ACKNOWLEDGEMENTS

There is no possible way I could ever be bold enough to write the Cake Chronicles 80/20 Healthy Relationship Challenge if it was not for the following people who helped me become the bold woman of God I am today

1. Giving all honor to God who is and has always been the head of my life.
2. To my husband Eddie Jr. (Mr. Cake) for all of the patience, dedication, and devotion he gives me in supporting the ongoing projects God inspires me to launch.
3. To my beautiful, wonderful, and amazing daughter Karie. God gave me more when he gave me you!
4. To "momma" my grandmother Mrs. Violetter VanHoose the original Mrs. Cake. Although she may not be here in her earthly form, she will FOREVER exist in my heart and I pray her wisdom will bless others as it has been a blessing to me.
5. To my mother, even though it was not her "desire" to teach me the meaning of dysfunction, I realize she is very wounded and her desire to fix others overshadows her ability to love herself.
6. To my RELATIVES who taught me how to redefine my definition of family by appreciating the people God put in my life who genuinely love me as "family" should.
7. To the person who caused the separation and discord in my family because they needed to hide their secrets. I have become a better human being because of you!
8. To my mother in love, Carolyn Brown for being obedient to the will of God and for loving me as her daughter while inspiring me to go to school to get my degree. She will FOREVER be appreciated, loved, and remembered.
9. To my father in love, Eddie Sr. for loving me as his daughter and for being the father I never had.
10. To my god parents George and Deborah for being the parent figures I needed and for checking in on me when the Holy Spirit told them too, which was always right on time.
11. To my niece Zarsha for designing and inspiring the Cake Chronicles logo.
12. To Zarsha and Jaz for being my models and to my youngest nieces Niana and Tiana for helping to promote my projects whenever they were asked.
13. To my Brown family, thank you for being the family I used to have and for supporting my projects over the years.
14. To Nilly, the person I loved as a sister and who was a "cheerleader" for me during the development of my projects.
15. To my sisters in love China and Rebekah. Thank you for being who you are in my life.
16. To the men of the Rochester Fatherhood Resource Initiative, Inc (RFRI) who loved, appreciated, and respected me for being who I was, and for teaching and showing me what real men looked like.
17. To the men who did not see my worth. God knew what was best!
18. To the companies I worked for who chose to fire me when I didn't deserve it. You helped me seek God's grace and mercy during the time of my storms.
19. To the many churches I have fellowshipped with. I learned how to seek God's purpose in my life even when I could not use my gifts at your church.
20. Most of all thank you for taking the time to read this book and to learn how to stop settling for the CRUMZ in life so you can achieve all that God desires for you .

MY MOTIVATION

My name is Delbra Brown and my grandmother's claim to fame was her ability to remember as far back in her childhood to the age of three, and her desire to tell jokes. She loved sharing her views about life and for her; she would use jokes and colloquial sayings to do so. One of her sayings when she wanted me to know that she was not going to just settle for less from anyone was "If I Can't Be The Cake, Damn the Crumbs". And whenever I introduced a guy to the family, instead of her telling me she didn't like him, she would just say "The First Month's Sugar, The Second Month's Pie, Third Month go to Hell, Damn You, and Die". As I got older, I realized her jokes and sayings were not just funny, but were used to teach me how to be prepared for life's issues. I found so much wisdom in her jokes and sayings that I decided to write them all down and today I have recorded over 100 of them, but when I found myself dealing with the trials and tribulations of dating, I would always remember these two sayings because she always quoted them when she wanted me to know she didn't like the guy I was dating.

From the age of 22 until I was 42, I was a single Christian woman growing up in what was and still is a "dysfunctional" family. Regardless of my family dynamics, I always knew there was something "special" about me. Yet like so many others growing up in an unhealthy environment, I could not put my finger on exactly what it was. I knew I didn't have the gifts of an entertainer or an athlete so I knew I would not impact the world in those areas, but I knew one day I would impact the world in my own way. When it came to relationships, I struggled with the same challenges as other single women such as having a child out of wedlock, trying to establish a healthy, long lasting relationship, while at the same time establishing an environment in my home where the dysfunctions I experienced as a child did not exist. After years of dating Mr. Wrong, when I turned 38, I finally decided to find out what "men" really thought about women, so I interviewed a few single men with the overall goal of understanding their views and opinions about love and relationships. I created a list of 90 questions I thought women would want to know and I polled a small group of men who were between the ages of 19 and 60 with the list of questions. One by one, as I interviewed them, I discovered they all felt the same way about all of the questions. That revelation fascinated me because I knew when it came to women, we would have 25 different answers to 10 questions. When I reflected on the interviews from the bachelors, my views about dating, and the "wisdom" of my grandmother's sayings, I began to realize that relationships are complicated because we have not been taught HOW to communicate effectively with one another. The goal of the *Cake Chronicles 80/20 Healthy Relationship Challenge* is to help women discover the ingredients and the work needed to establish a healthy, loving, Godly relationship with others. And at the same time, not lose site of who they are and what they need to be happy. The information compiled in this book is a compilation of 30+ years of my personal trials and tribulations of dating; along with the wisdom God led me to discover about this issue in my desire to identify solutions to these challenges.

IF I CAN'T BE THE CAKE, I WON'T BE THE CRUMZ

OUTLINE

WHAT IS THE CAKE CHRONICLES 80/20 RELATIONSHIP CHALLENGE?
- What is the 80/20 Relationship Challenge? ………..……......……..09
- Consequences of the Fall………………..…..….……..…….……..10
- The "Struggle" To Be Holy………………….…..…….….………..11
- Church Folks vs Christians………..……………….………….……13
- The 7 Principles of Wisdom………………..…….……….………..15
- Are you ready to be Transformed?……………………...…………..16
- Applying God's Principles In Our Lives………………….………..17
- Dealing with the Issues of Life………….…………….……..……..18
- Transformation (The Process To Long Lasting Change)…..,.….…..19
- Keep Doing, Start Doing, and Stop Doing………..……..…….…...20
- Poem - Boundaries (Riah 2017)..………..………….….…..….…..22

WHY ARE RELATIONSHIPS "HARD"
- There's More Below the Surface………………….……….……...24
  - ⇒ 1. Breaking Life Long Habits………………….……….…….25
  - ⇒ 2. Understanding "Dysfunctional" Relationships……….…..…..26
  - ⇒ 3. Exactly What Is "Self-Esteem?"……………….…….……...27
  - ⇒ 4) Do you really "Hear Me"……………….….……...………..28
  - ⇒ 5) Communication, Communication, Communication …..….…..29
  - ⇒ 6) The Frog in the Pot Analogy…....….……….…..…….……..30
  - ⇒ 7) Power & Control………………….……..……..……….…..31
- Poem - Relationships are Hard (Riah 2017)……………….….……36

CAKE POP - SELF LOVE
- What Do You Need To Be Happy (What Is Your 80/20)?…………..38
  - ⇒ 1. Avoid "Icing" Type Relationships………….…….…....……..39
  - ⇒ 2. Getting Your Emotional Needs Met……...………..…….…..40
  - ⇒ 3. Your Life Map………….………..…………………………..41
  - ⇒ 4. What is your Definition of Love?…..……….….…….…...…..42
  - ⇒ 5. Establishing "Boundaries" and "Balance"……….….….……..43
  - ⇒ 6. What is Your Love Language?…….….……….….…….……..44
  - ⇒ 7. Unhealthy Communication Styles….…………….……...…..45
  - ⇒ 8. Codependent Tendencies……………….……..……….……..46
  - ⇒ 9. Words Not to Say…….….……….….…….….……….……..47
  - ⇒ 10. Are you Passive or Aggressive?…..………….……..……...48
  - ⇒ 11. Understanding Your Feelings & Emotions……..…………..49
- Poem - OleSelfLove (Mariah 2017)..……….….…….…….……..50

IF I CAN'T BE THE CAKE, I WON'T BE THE CRUMZ

OUTLINE

CUP CAKE - RELATIONSHIPS WITH OTHERS
- Are you ready for a Relationship?..56
  ⇒ 1. What is "Revelation" in a Relationship?.…..............................57
  ⇒ 2. My Grandmother's Three (3) Month Relationship Rule……………..……..58
  ⇒ 3. Are They Worthy of Your Heart?..59
  ⇒ 4. Identifying a Man Worthy of Your Heart...................................60
  ⇒ 5. Identifying a Godly Man………………………………..…….....…62
  ⇒ 6. Men are Definitely From Mars……………………………………….63
  ⇒ 7. Getting Him to Listen When You Talk………………..……..……….64
  ⇒ 8. Submission?……………………………………………….……...65
- Poem - Hello Friend (Riah 2017)………………………………………….70

MRS CAKE - I'M MARRIED…………………………………………….71
- What is Marriage?..72
- Dealing with Blended Families………………………………………....73
- Dealing with Extended Family Members……………………………….74
- The Proverbs 31 Woman…..75
- Proverbs 31 Woman - To Herself……..75
- Proverbs 31 Woman - To Her Husband………………………………….78
- Proverbs 31 Woman - To Her Family……………………………..…….80
- Proverbs 31 Woman - To Others……………………………………….82
- Virtuous Woman Checklist……………………………………………...84
- Poem - God Gave Me More (*Lu Highsmith*)…………………..……...88

CRUMZY SITUATIONS - IT'S "COMPLICATED"
- What are CRUMZY Situations…………………………………..……...90
  ⇒ Staying for the Children or for Money …………………...............91
  ⇒ Separated or Married But Living Like You're Single………………92
  ⇒ What is Intimate Partner Violence (IPV)………………..…………93
  ⇒ Domestic Violence………………………………..……………….94
  ⇒ Bullying vs. Stalking……………………..……..………………...95

OUTLINE

CRUMZY SITUATIONS - IT'S "COMPLICATED"
- ⇒ Dealing with Undeserved Rejection from Others..................96
- ⇒ Dealing with Rejection you Deserved to Receive................97
- ⇒ Parents Who Won't Let Go....................................98
- ⇒ Parents "Demanding" Respect from their Adult Children.........99
- ⇒ Irresponsible Parents.......................................100
- ⇒ Dealing with Disrespectful Children.........................101
- ⇒ Dealing with Baby Daddy/Momma Issues........................102
- ⇒ Adults Depending on Other People............................103
- ⇒ Friendships vs. Acquaintances - Know the difference.........104
- ⇒ Family vs. Relatives..105
- ⇒ Respect vs. Disrespect......................................106
- ⇒ Common Sense Is Not So Common Anymore.......................107
- ⇒ The Pitfalls of Online Dating/Cat fishing...................108
- ⇒ Dealing with Loved ones with Mental/Drug Addiction..........109
- ⇒ Not Appreciating/Disrespecting Good Men.....................110
- ⇒ Loaning Money to Friends/Family.............................111
- ⇒ Generational "Habits" Not "Curses"..........................112
- ⇒ Not Knowing YOU MATTER......................................113
- ⇒ Not Being Prepared for Life Transitions.....................114
- ⇒ Truth vs. Lies..115
- ⇒ Relationships with People Incarcerated......................116
- ⇒ Love vs. Lust...117
- • Poem - I've Had Enough (Riah 2017).........................112

CRUMZ SNATCHER - SIDE CHICK..................................121
- • Crumz Snatcher...122
- • Poem - I Deserve Better (Riah 2017)........................128

SUMMARY..129
- • Poem - We Are The Women (Riah 2017)........................130
- • When You've Done All You Can...............................131

REFERENCES...132

IF I CAN'T BE THE CAKE, I WON'T BE THE CRUMZ

WHAT IS THE CAKE CHRONICLES 80/20 HEALTHY RELATIONSHIP CHALLENGE?

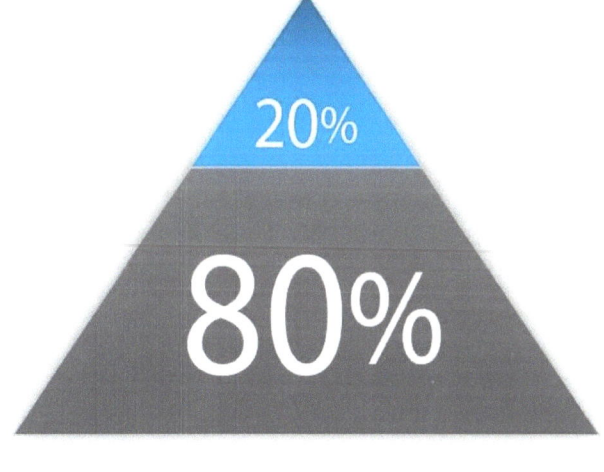

THE TRUE BEAUTY OF A WOMAN

Beautifully and Wonderfully made I know that, will live that and that's a fact too

Living my truth of how I was created in my Beauty of me and not you,

I looked in the mirror and who did I see
A beautiful woman looking back at me.

Hair rollers, face cream and sleep in my eyes
Give me an half-hour you will be surprised.

Transformed, make over a do me in my beauty you see
Same girl, same woman, natural hair, permed if I like, even lipsticks, mascara, a new doo that's me.

Just love being a woman, just love being me,
just love looking in my mirror and Just Love The Beautiful Me.

So before I can Love you, I have to Love me
And it starts with learning my 80/20 because that helps me
To know who I am and appreciate "whose" I am.

By Riah (2017)

WHAT IS THE 80/20 RELATIONSHIP CHALLENGE

      I do not proclaim to be an expert in religion, psychology, or counseling, but experience and my dysfunctional family have taught me a lot about all three. My family migrated from the South in search of a better life, but the women in my family did not set a "great" example of healthy relationships because they themselves did not experience one. My step father was emotionally, psychologically, and physically abusive so I could not look to my mother for advice about relationships because I saw her settling for less in her own. My youngest aunt was only 13 years older than me so she felt as if she was just as "young" as I was so I never really had a relationship with her. My oldest aunt was a wonderfully, amazing woman who loved everyone but she only had sons. Therefore, growing up during the 80s and 90s as my mother's oldest and only daughter, as well as being the oldest female in my family wasn't easy, Being the oldest and only girl, not having "healthy females guide me as I encountered different life challenges, when it came down to my figuring out what a healthy loving relationship was, I was on my own. Like most adults in the 80s and 90s, I learned how to establish relationships by watching others on television and in movies. One day while watching the movie *"Why Did I Get Married"*, written by Tyler Perry, a group of married couples went on a retreat and one of the guys invited his "side chick". When the group of men asked their friend why he brought his "other woman" knowing their wives would be there, one of the guys told them about the 80/20 rule. He stated the 80/20 rule was when a man would leave an 80 (a good woman) for a 20 (something he thinks is better than what he has). As I thought about what he said, and questioned the truth behind that statement, I knew one day I would figure out why that was the case.

      When I turned 38 I asked God to help me understand why dating and relationships were so complicated. As He revealed the answer to me, and as I used the knowledge to help me fix my relationship issues, I wanted to find a unique way to help others so I decided to use my grandmother's sayings, cake, and that 80/20 rule to encourage others to strive for happiness in their life. As I worked with my family and friends to develop the different "cake" type of relationships, and as I thought about different "crumzy" situations, I remembered that conversation from the movie, and I began to understand why a person would be willing to jeopardize what they have (the Cake or their 80%) for something that looks better or appears to be better (Icing, a CRUMZY situation or their 20%). When you no longer "value" the relationship you have or you don't think the person you're with is capable of making you happy, you start sabotaging what you have by searching for something "better". When you have never been taught how to define what happiness means to you, you will chase something or someone else even if you know it won't last. Once I understood that theory, the Cake Chronicles 80/20 Healthy Relationship Challenge was born. In order for you to know that you're mate can fulfill your needs, you first have to know **WHAT YOUR NEEDS ARE**! The 80 is the minimum you need and require, and the 20 is what you can compromise or let go.

CONSEQUENCES OF THE FALL

The book of Genesis in the Bible is an account of the first husband and wife who had a "communication" problem. God specifically told Adam what his expectations were for him and Eve. However, when Eve asked Adam to eat from the forbidden tree, what she was really asking him to do was to purposely and knowingly go against the will of the Lord. Instead of Adam reflecting on God's commandments to them, he decided to listen to Eve and thus, sin entered into the world. Adam and Eve's desire to be disobedient, along with their inability to hear and respect God's commandments caused mankind to experience hardship as a result of their actions and desires to go against God and His commandments. Like Adam and Eve, we struggle to maintain healthy communication strategies in our relationships because Adam and Eve failed to "obey" the will of God. When they chose to go against God, they introduced doubt, uncertainty, trust issues, and disobedience into their relationship with one another, and their relationship with God, which in turn causes mankind to experience those same unhealthy behaviors with one another.

Christian women may face challenges in their relationships when they strive to apply Godly principles in their life, while at the same adopting worldly characteristics, and behaviors. In order for women to do what the Lord wants for their lives, they have to take a step back and start reflecting on exactly what that is. It is not enough knowing who God is. Salvation comes from hearing, believing, acknowledging, and accepting the word of God. Then transformation occurs when you adopt His principles and then apply them into your daily walk. Once you are saved, the transformation process is where the real work begins. Relationships with others are just like your relationship with God. The first step is acceptance. Healthy, happy, loving relationships occur when you apply healthy, Godly principles in the way you communicate with others on a daily basis! In order to define your 80/20, you have to understand how to be healed and delivered from your unhealthy habits. Which mean you have to die of your fleshly ways "daily" and pick up more Christ like behavior and characteristics. Establishing boundaries is a necessity, and in order to be delivered; you have to believe and accept God's principles as the key to your healing.

THE "STRUGGLE" TO BE HOLY

Many times, the struggle to be "holy" is more about the person's understanding or interpretation about what is considered a "sin." Do you accept the sin because others say it is okay, or do you believe what the Bible says about it? Before the 1960's a sinner would do what they did behind closed doors, and only a few people would know about it. Because of technology and social media, sin has become "normalized" or considered acceptable because the world wants you to believe you can do whatever you want and it is "okay." Television and social media should never be your gauge or example of what is morally acceptable and appropriate behavior as a Christian.

[10] As it is written: "There is no one righteous, not even one;
[11] there is no one who understands, no one who seeks God.
[12] All have turned away, they have together become worthless; there is no one who does good, not even one."
[13] "Their throats are open graves; their tongues practice deceit." "The poison of vipers is on their lips."
[14] "Their mouths are full of cursing and bitterness."
[15] "Their feet are swift to shed blood;
[16] ruin and misery mark their ways,
[17] and the way of peace they do not know."
[18] "There is no fear of God before their eyes."
[19] Now we know that whatever the law says, it says to those who are under the law, so that every mouth may be silenced and the whole world held accountable to God.
[20] Therefore no one will be declared righteous in his sight by observing the law; rather, through the law we become conscious of sin.
[21] But now a righteousness from God, apart from law, has been made known, to which the Law and the Prophets testify.
[22] This righteousness from God comes through faith in Jesus Christ to all who believe. There is no difference,
[23] for all have sinned and fall short of the glory of God,
[24] and are justified freely by his grace through the redemption that came by Christ Jesus.
[25] God presented him as a sacrifice of atonement, through faith in his blood. He did this to demonstrate his justice, because in his forbearance he had left the sins committed beforehand unpunished (Romans 3:10-26).

12 The night is nearly over; the day is almost here. So let us put aside the deeds of darkness and put on the armor of light. 13 Let us behave decently, as in the daytime, not in orgies and drunkenness, not in sexual immorality and debauchery, not in dissension and jealousy. 14 Rather, clothe yourselves with the Lord Jesus Christ, and do not think about how to gratify the desires of the sinful nature (Romans 13:12-14).

IF I CAN'T BE THE CAKE, I WON'T BE THE CRUMZ

THE "STRUGGLE" TO BE HOLY
continued

<u>*Put to death, therefore, whatever belongs to your earthly nature*</u> *(Col 3:5-10)*

21For although they knew God, they neither glorified him as God nor gave thanks to him, but their thinking became futile and their foolish hearts were darkened. <u>*22Although they claimed to be wise, they became fools 23and exchanged the glory of the immortal God for images made to look like a mortal human being and birds and animals and reptiles.*</u> *24 Therefore* **God gave them over in the sinful desires of their hearts to sexual impurity for the degrading of their bodies with one another. 25They exchanged the truth about God for a lie, and worshiped and served created things rather than the Creator—who is forever praised. Amen***. 26Because of this,* <u>*God gave them over to shameful lusts. Even their women exchanged natural sexual relations for unnatural ones.*</u> *27 In the same way the* <u>*men also abandoned natural relations with women and were inflamed with lust for one another. Men committed shameful acts with other men, and received in themselves the due penalty for their error. 28 And even as they did not like to retain God in their knowledge, God gave them over to a reprobate mind, to do those things which are not convenient; 29 Being filled with all unrighteousness, fornication, wickedness, covetousness, maliciousness; full of envy, murder, debate, deceit, malignity; whisperers,30 Backbiters, haters of God, despiteful, proud, boasters, inventors of evil things, disobedient to parents,31 Without understanding, covenant breakers, without natural affection, implacable, unmerciful:*</u>*32* **Who knowing the judgment of God, that they which commit such things are worthy of death, not only do the same, but have pleasure in them that do them***. For the acts of the sinful nature are obvious (Romans 1:21-32)*

But now I am writing you that you must not associate with anyone who Calls himself a brother with such a man do not even eat (1 Corinthians 5:11).

Do you not know that the wicked will not inherit the kingdom of God? Do not be deceived: I warn you, as I did before that those who live like this will not inherit the kingdom of God (1 Corinthians 6:9-10)

      If someone says they're a Christian and yet, they are behaving in a Carnal fashion, when you say something to them and you don't base your comments or perceptions on the word of God, they will say you are "judging" them. The only true conviction of what is morally right and acceptable is the Bible and the Holy Spirit. Be sure to base your views and opinions on the word of God and not of your emotions and feelings. The word, is the word, is the word. Standing on the word and the truth of God is the only way to help those who "accept" God, desire to live according to his word, and NOT the God of their imagination.

CHURCH FOLKS VS. CHRISTIANS

In the Bible, Paul spoke about three types of people: The Natural Man, The Carnal Man, and The Spiritual Man.

The Natural Man: This is the person that has not received Christ or who has chosen not to acknowledge Jesus Christ as their Lord and Savior. The "Natural Man" or those who choose to live their lives governed by their emotions and their fleshly desires feel justified in doing whatever feels right for them and to them. [1] *"As for you, you were dead in your transgressions and sins,* [2] *You used to live just like the rest of the world, full of sin, obeying Satan, the mighty prince of the power of the air. He is the spirit at work in the hearts of those who refuse to obey God.* [3] *All of us used to live that way, following the passions and desires of our evil nature. We were born with an evil nature, and we were under God's anger just like everyone else (Ephesians 2:1-3)"*. It is difficult trying to help people who have no regard for moral principles concerning what is right or wrong, or acceptable behavior because for them **everything** is acceptable and every human being has the right to do what they choose to do; good, bad or indifferent. *"But the natural man receiveth not the things of the Spirit of God: for they are foolishness unto him: neither can he know them, because they are spiritually discerned (1 Corinthians 2:14)"*.

The Carnal Man: In the Book of Galatians, Paul also tells us about the Carnal Man; *"And I, brethren, could not speak unto you as unto spiritual, but as unto carnal, even as unto babes in Christ (KJV 1 Corinthians 3:1). For ye are yet carnal: for whereas there is among you envying, and strife, and divisions, are ye not carnal, and walk as men (KJV 1 Corinthians 3:3)?"*

Paul also lists the works of the flesh in his writing to the Galatians; *"Now the works of the flesh are manifest, which are these; Adultery, fornication, uncleanness, lasciviousness (KJV Galatians 5:19), idolatry, witchcraft, hatred, variance, emulations, wrath, strife, seditions, heresies (KJV Galatians 5:20), envying, murders, drunkenness, revellings, and such like: of the which I tell you before, as I have also told you in time past, that they which do such things shall not inherit the kingdom of God (KJV Galatians 5:21)"*.

CHURCH FOLKS VS. CHRISTIANS
continued

In these verses, Paul states they are "babes in Christ", which mean he recognizes they accept who God is, but he knows he can't speak to them about the things of the spirit, because their actions were "carnal". The carnal man receives Jesus Christ as his Lord and Savior; yet he lives his life like he hasn't. Their behavior models that of carnality. We all know a few people who live like this. They go to church, read their Bible, and can even hold an "intelligent" conversation with other believers about faith while at the same time they live their life as though they do not know who Jesus Christ. They are carnal in their thoughts and ways thus **The Carnal Minded Christian.** Today, Carnal Minded Christians always try to "justify" their actions by saying *"we know we all fall short, and that we are forgiven of our sins,"* yet as a Christian they keep forgetting that the 1st step to being saved is repenting of your sins. When we let go, but then pick up the sin and the behavior that is not becoming of a Christian, time after time, again and again, in those moments we find ourselves engaging in carnal behavior thus the label Carnal Minded Christians. This behavior is at the heart of what separates Church Folks vs Christians. Church folks know God and believe in His word, but yet they do and say what they want to. Christians are mindful of God's will for their lives and allow the Holy Spirit to convict them when their actions are contrary to God's will. That is the difference. It is not our job to judge. It is better to see church folks at least go to church, than to choose to disregard who He is. TV shows depict messages about "church folks" because it's easier to make you believe all God fearing, Bible, believers act that way. We must let our light shine so that others can see who He really is and not the Carnal depiction of Christians that non believers want people to see.

Spiritual Maturity. The word "Spiritual" deals with your health while "Maturity" deals with your growth. God wants you to grow. We are designed to grow. Spiritual Maturity is a journey that one embarks upon but is never ending. Though we may never reach a complete level of Spiritual Maturity –we should always be in a process of learning, growing, and striving to be Christ Like. Our level of spiritual maturity is also displayed through our Christ-Like behavior with everyone we come in contact with on a day to day basis. Your levels of blessings are based on your level of maturity and capabilities *(Matthew 25.15, Galatians 4.1-3)*, and your level of growth is based on your desire to grow *(1 Peter 2.1)*. Your spiritual growth is not based on the knowledge you have obtained, but in your works, deeds, behavior, and beliefs. I like to use the phrase "Don't Talk About It, Be About It" (Romans 12:2).

Different

THE SEVEN PRINCIPLES OF WISDOM

Once you have accepted Jesus Christ as your Lord and Savior, the journey towards living as the "Spiritual man" includes understanding the seven principles to obtaining Wisdom:

1) Knowledge: Once we are saved (or reborn) this is the beginning of our journey where God expects us to grow and mature as Christians. This is done through growing in the knowledge of who God, the Holy Spirit, Jesus Christ is, and in reading the Word.

2) Fear: Is having a deep reverence in God. For this is the first step towards having true wisdom. The fear of him is more about respect, and acceptance than being emotionally afraid.

3) Mindful: When you are mindful of who God is, you're sensitive to the Holy Spirit and your mind is set to love and obey God.

4) Understanding: You strive to have an understanding of God gained by comprehending His Will for your life.

5) Trust: Absolute unwavering belief.

6) Obedience: Willingly submitting to God's authority.

7) Transformation: Your transformation begins when you are no longer governed by the old nature that's led by the flesh (emotions, feelings, and sight). But you are led by the Holy Spirit and accept the new nature and not led by just your emotions.

This is gained through **knowledge** and the teachings of God, the Holy Spirit and Jesus Christ. Having **fear** of God means to show a deep reverence for Him. For this is the first step towards having true wisdom. When we are **mindful** of God, we are sensitive to the Holy Spirit and our mind is set to love and obey God. To understand God means having the knowledge gained through the process of comprehending and **trusting** willingly with absolute unwavering belief that we will submit to God's Authority.

WHAT IS THE 80/20 RELATIONSHIP CHALLENGE

ARE YOU READY TO BE TRANSFORMED?

In the Bible, Jesus spoke in parables, or earthly stories which have a Heavenly meaning. The parable of the Sower and the Seed in Matthew 13:1 - 23, helps us understand there will be 1) people who do not want to believe in God, 2) people who want to believe but when they try to do the work that is needed to live their life as a Christian start to feel it's "too hard" so they give up, and then 3) the person who gets it and is willing to do the work needed to apply His principles willingly into their life. That parable helped me understand not everyone will be able to do the work that is needed to establish a healthy, loving, relationship with others based on Christian principles so just like the parable, I group individuals into three categories:

Person 1 - No Growth. This person does not want to change anything in their life or do the work that is needed to change their unhealthy learned habits, so they find themselves being content with living miserably.

Person 2 - Wants growth, but experiences the same thing over and over again and is not quite sure how to stop the madness. They want and desire to get off the merry-go-round of crazy, but they are not quite sure how.

Person 3 - Seeks knowledge, and even though it is difficult to the do the work required to change, they choose not to give up.

Like the parable of the Sower and the Seed, ask yourself which person do you want to be? Change is hard, because it took a lifetime to establish your "unhealthy habits" and behaviors. However, with the right frame of mine, you can *"Do all things through Christ who strengthens you" (Philippians 4:13)."* Keep in mind however, that just because you "believe" what you are doing is God's will for your life, does not necessarily mean it is. If you believe in your heart that God is a God of infinite wisdom who knows what is best for your life, when you are denied something you wanted or even prayed about, you won't be hurt, depressed, or sad when you don't get it. Instead, you can see it as something you are either not ready to receive "at this time", or it wasn't what was best for you. Pray, asking God for His will to be done in your life about that situation, and then surrender it to Him. If it is His will for you, then it will be. If it is not, then be patient while you are waiting for His will to be revealed and done.

IF I CAN'T BE THE CAKE, I WON'T BE THE CRUMZ

WHAT IS THE 80/20 RELATIONSHIP CHALLENGE

APPLYING GOD'S PRINCIPLES IN OUR LIVES

There are three standing elements in our lives.

1) **Faith**
2) **Men and**
3) **Women.**

Everything in life is centered around making decisions based on these elements with God and your faith at the head of the triangle, and men and women on each end. Our decisions are focused around seven principles which are found in the center of the triangle:

1. **Society** - understanding the issues you face influenced by society's impact on your life.
2. **Family** - understanding the issues you face daily centered around your family dynamics.
3. **Self** - you must understand who you are as an individual who has your own desires, wants and needs.
4. **Relationships** - understanding the challenges you face with friends, coworkers and loved ones.
5. **Parenting** - understanding your roles as a parent.
6. **Finances** - learning how to become a great steward with your finances.
7. **Faith** - understand God's role in all areas of your life.

The greatest challenge you can face as a Christian is maintaining "balance" while applying God in all seven of these areas. When you work daily to do that, you become one with Him and as a Christian, you should strive to achieve BALANCE.

IF I CAN'T BE THE CAKE, I WON'T BE THE CRUMZ

WHAT IS THE 80/20 RELATIONSHIP CHALLENGE

DEALING WITH THE ISSUES OF LIFE

The reason life seems difficult to manage or balance is because you are at the center managing all of the decisions in these seven areas and because they usually intertwine and overlap one another, it feels as if you can never get a break from them. If God gave them to you, then He will get you through them. If you brought them on yourself, He is still there willing and able to help you deal with them but you have to invite him into the process.

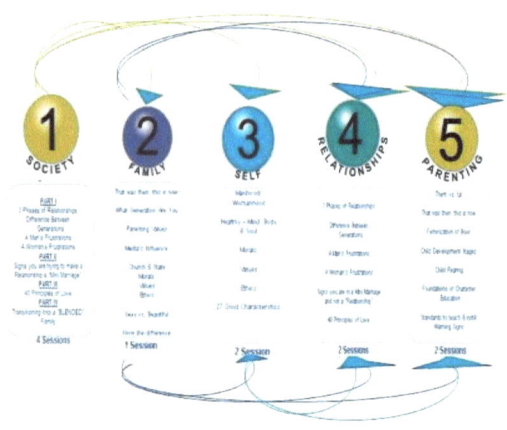

TRANSFORMATION
THE PROCESS TO LONG LASTING CHANGE

The true process of Transformation is one's ability to use wisdom for God's purpose and His glory while applying it to all areas of your life.

Once we have been transformed, we can now walk in Spiritual Maturity and

1) Not be drawn into jealousy and strife *(James 3:16)*

2) Train yourself to discern the difference between good and evil *(Hebrews 5:14),*

3) Actively and aggressively pursue Transformation *(Philippians 3:12-15, Ephesians 4:22-24).*

4) Have a sense of stability a) Knowing who the God you serve really is; b) Not living in bondage to anyone; c) Your identity: you know who you are as a child of God; d) in their emotions: you are not emotionally ruled which may cause you to react based on feelings and not on what is morally or spiritually right; e) and your speech. For you know there is power in the words you speak and so you are cautious in what you say and how it is said.

IF I CAN'T BE THE CAKE, I WON'T BE THE CRUMZ

TRANSFORMATION
THE PROCESS TO LONG LASTING CHANGE
continued

1) Strive to fulfill your purpose and don't make excuses

2) You are not afraid to receive correction or instruction or rebukes for not clearly understanding an issue

3) Esteem the things of God higher than the things of this world and

4) You are able to recognize when God is at work in a situation or circumstance.

5) Receive the correction of the Holy Spirit whenever it is given

      The purpose of this workbook is to help you understand why relationships are complicated and the work it will take for you to discover what you need to be happy, so you can see if the people in your life deserve your heart. Like a workout coach, this 80/20 Healthy Relationship Challenge is designed to change and stretch your perception about relationships and help you achieve the love, peace, and happiness you desire. In order to do that, you must apply **Christ like behavior in how you relate to others, and how they relate to you.** As you read each section of this book do the following:

REFLECT: Ask yourself if it will be a challenge for you to not exhibit this behavior, and what or who causes you to experience challenges with not exhibiting this characteristic/behavior

REVEAL: If you find it to be a challenge, then prayerfully ask the Lord to reveal to you through the Holy Spirit what or who makes it challenging for you to change. Also through talking with others, meditation and prayer, ask the Lord to reveal to you what you should stop doing in order to exhibit the characteristics and behaviors outlined in the scriptures

HEAL: Then prayerfully ask the Lord to help you surrender you're acceptance for doing those things so that you can adopt the characteristics and behavior of Christ, walk in the will of God, and represent yourself as a true Christian and not that of a Carnal-Minded Christian.

KEEP DOING, START DOING, AND STOP DOING

In my professional life as a Quality Engineer or a Tester. I work with a team of others to ensure the design and implementation of software is sound based on the business requesting the work, and the customers who will be using the application. There is a methodology called Agile which encourages the team to implement efficient processes in order to achieve these goals and at the end of the sprint or the designed project time frame, the team reflects on the implementation of their work and discuss what worked well and what they are doing that should be changed. This same methodology works great in applying these principles in our everyday lives, so at the end of each section use the pages provided to reflect on your behavior and how you can work towards identifying your 80/20 for that area. You will be asked to identify the following:

KEEP

What should I continue doing that is working well and supports my goals in this area

START

What do I need to start doing to ensure I exemplify the healthy, positive behavior outlined

STOP

What do I need to stop doing that is hindering me from making healthy, positive choices in this area

WHAT IS THE 80/20 RELATIONSHIP CHALLENGE

    Women are not taught how to identify what they need to be happy or their **80%** and thus they date people without taking the time to see if the person is even qualified to be given the time of day, let alone their heart. Because there is no perfect person other than Jesus Christ, you have to be willing to "compromise" and accept some things that you might not want too. This is your **20%**. When you do not know what you need, you spend a great deal of time trying to turn a 20 into an 80. That might work for some people, but 9 times out of 10 you will have to put a lot of work and effort into getting that person to be what you need and thus you may find yourself trying to CONTROL them. There is nothing wrong with compromising, but when you compromise more than the 20%, you start settling for less than your 80% and that is what causes you to be bitter, unhappy, unfulfilled, and unsatisfied. If you believe that God is in control over your life, then you must surrender and trust Him with this new process of learning how to define what He wants you to have especially in this area of how you date or relate with other people.

NO MORE PUTTING OTHERS FIRST

DEFINE WHAT YOU NEED TO BE HAPPY

*YOUR HAPPINESS IS NOT DEFINED
BY YOUR NEED TO MAKE OTHERS HAPPY
IT'S OKAY TO LOVE YOURSELF*

LOVE CHRIST

LOVE YOURSELF

LOVE OTHERS

THAT'S THE ORDER FOR BALANCE!

IF I CAN'T BE THE CAKE, I WON'T BE THE CRUMZ

BOUNDARIES

My brokenness and heartaches
I turned into strengths,
to challenge the steps that I now make

Loving you was not easy,
but I chose to love you
even in your mistakes.

With your burdens in my space
while wiping away your tears

Cried with you held your hand
while you conquered your fears.

Limiting me from me,
when I hear
the inner voice inside me crying

from the back bent scuffed knees,
and half opened eyes

I still answer to the call of your voice,
your whisper never in a disguise.

I am who I am,
and I will continue
to set boundaries for myself

I have to live in my struggles
turning them into victories.

I finally found that inner peace
that I cherish
from the unlimited spaces
you prepared

Now I seek refuge in my wisdom,
my comfort
from the broken heartaches
that we shared.
So, as I come to the close of this day
at this appointed time,
my journey to my end

Yes, I set boundaries for me
as I understand if you can't be my love
it may be best for to just be a friend

By Riah (2017)

IF I CAN'T BE THE CAKE, I WON'T BE THE CRUMZ

WHY ARE RELATIONSHIPS HARD?

WHY ARE RELATIONSHIPS "HARD"

THERE'S MORE BELOW THE SURFACE

When you base your decisions by what you "see," you miss what lies below the surface. One reason relationships are hard is because people don't realize how much effort is required to establish a healthy and loving one. You can't judge a book by it's cover, and you definitely can't determine if someone is right for you based only on what you can see. You have to give the relationship some time in order for you to truly dig deep below the surface to learn who they really are, and if who they are compliments who you are. We all have a story to tell, and our life journey and experiences are not all the same, therefore you have to;

1) slow down and take your time getting to know who the real person is,
2) learn how to read the person so that you can discover who they really are so
3) you can determine if they are worthy of your heart and your time.

Many times people jump into a "situation" before they have done the work that is needed to build a relationship with a foundation that can stand the test of time. When a person believes they attract and are attracted to the same type of person, they are actually choosing to accept that type of person because they believe they will understand them and make them happy. But when you discover your choices in partners is not working the way you desired, you have to determine why you are attracted to that type of person. Insanity is defined as doing the same thing over and over again, expecting different results. This definition applies to this situation. You won't get different results if you don't learn how to think, and be different with your relationship habits. The first step is to 1) understand why you are attracted to "unhealthy" behavior in people, 2) discover what you need to do to change your behavior, 3) do the work that is needed to change, 4) learn how to read others, 5) set boundaries with the people in your life who do not line up with what you need.

Determine your 80%
Determine your 20%
Never settle for less than 80/20

Appreciate the people in your life who fulfill at least 80% of your needs. When you learn how to think in this fashion, you begin to appreciate the people in your life who genuinely care for you. Until you change how you think about relationships, you will continue to attract unhealthy ones so the first step in changing your unhealthy behavior is learning what is considered unhealthy!

IF I CAN'T BE THE CAKE, I WON'T BE THE CRUMZ

1. BREAKING LIFE LONG HABITS

  Katt Williams the comedian tried his best to tell women during a stand up routine that "Self-Esteem" is the "ESTEEM OF YOURSELF". What he was emphatically trying to say is that women need to realize that loving yourself starts with the person you see in the mirror. You have to stop looking for others to validate you or desire for them to always tell you what you want to hear, instead of what you need to hear. The mistake people don't understand about the word self-esteem is we are not taught or expected to think about what we want to be happy. Especially caregivers and nurturers who find it hard to put their needs ahead of others. When men are not equipped financially to take care of themselves, they prey on women by looking for those who look like they enjoy being "Mrs. Fix It". Men determine which women to prey on by "reading" them and looking for women who look like they will do anything for love. When a woman grows up in a household where she never felt like her thoughts, views, opinions, and desires mattered, she will become a woman who is attracted to men and people in need of someone to take care of them because she is trying to replace the love she feels she has not received as a child.

  Unfortunately, **HURT PEOPLE HURT PEOPLE**. The concept behind this saying can be found in the research you will discover on the topic of self-esteem. When people are hurting, or they are trying to keep their personal secret a "secret", they hurt you first, or deflect the conversation to keep from addressing the real problem. In other words, they **HURT YOU** before you can **HURT THEM**. Men who grew up in in a dysfunctional household or one where they did not grow up with a healthy father figure to teach them how to love and care for women as God intended, become hurt men who hurt the women and children in their lives because they are also dealing with the same or similar hurtful childhood experiences. The first step in understanding how to stop being victimized is to evaluate your good and bad habits and ask yourself where they were derived from. When you're longing for something, you chase it the hardest. Unhealthy behaviors practiced repeatedly over time become unhealthy life habits. The reason habits are difficult to break is because of the electrical pulses and signals in your brain, which have become conditioned to perform the tasks, you have trained them to perform. Over time, they become a part of your routine. In order to break them, you have to re-train your brain to expect a different response and behavior.

WHY ARE RELATIONSHIPS "HARD"

2. UNDERSTANDING "DYSFUNCTIONAL RELATIONSHIPS"

According to Wikipedia "*A dysfunctional family is a family in which conflict, misbehavior, and often child neglect or abuse on the part of individual parents occur continually and regularly, leading other members to accommodate such actions. Children sometimes grow up in such families with the understanding that such an arrangement is normal. Dysfunctional families are primarily a result of co-dependent adults, and may also be affected by addictions, such as substance abuse (e.g., alcohol or drugs), or sometimes an untreated mental illness.*" A person who lives in a home either as a child, or in a dysfunctional environment as an adult grows up feeling as though their needs, wants and desires can't be met by others because their focus is on caring for others before they take care of themselves. When you live in this type of environment, your definition of love is based on your need to **take care of others**, over **caring for yourself**. In order for you to establish "healthier" relationships with others, you must first understand how living in a dysfunctional environment negatively effects you. Unhealthy, dysfunctional behavior is not "new" as it has been in existence since the beginning of time since with Adam and Eve. The Bible calls individuals who create and accept dysfunctional lifestyles "Carnal Minded Christians. This book *"Breaking Free"* was the first of many books the Lord revealed to me that helped me understand how the "issues" in my life were not my fault, and I was not the problem. Hurting adults, are actually wounded children.

BOOK TABLE OF CONTENTS

The Dysfunctional Family
The Victim Personality
The Victim Triangle
The Victim Triangle and Sexual Abuse
The Victim Triangle and Family Abuse
The Addictive/Alcoholic Family
The Victim Triangle and domestic Abuse
I Can't Stop
The Victim Personality Out of Control
Treatment of Victim Patterns
Changing the Pattern of Rescuing
Healing the Persecutor Personality
The Personal Transformation Intensive
The Healing of the Victim Reuniting With the Child Within

Diane Zimberoff, Breaking Free from the Victim Trap: Reclaiming Your Personal Power, Wellness Press; 5th (2011) edition (November 7, 2011)

IF I CAN'T BE THE CAKE, I WON'T BE THE CRUMZ

WHY ARE RELATIONSHIPS "HARD"

3. EXACTLY WHAT IS "SELF-ESTEEM?"

When I was 38 and still single, I realized I was not sure what men really wanted in relationships, so I decided to interview some single bachelors to ask them 98 questions I compiled to get their views about dating, relationships and marriage. One of the bachelors (who was 59 at the time) asked me *"Why do women have such low self-esteem?"* I knew I personally did not have low self-esteem because I thought rather highly of myself. However, I knew the women he dated were very educated and for him to feel this way about them intrigued me, so the question warranted deeper thought, reflection, and research about why he felt that way. That night I woke up at 4:00 am and I decided to search online for some books about self-esteem and the Lord directed me to the book *"Self Esteem and Getting Ahead."* After ordering and reading it, I discovered when a person does not have a "healthy" understanding and love of themselves, they lash out on others and unknowingly make people feel bad because they are hurting and dealing with their own issues. This deflective, destructive behavior lies at the core of low self-worth, and low self-esteem. When you understand the five components of self-esteem; **1) Self-Worth, 2) Self-Image, 3) Self-Respect, and 4) Self-Confidence,** you learn how to read others and how to set boundaries when they try to make you feel guilty for their short-comings. Take the time to learn what self-esteem really is. Once you have an understanding of self-esteem, you can identify the areas within yourself that you are struggling with so you can pray and ask God to strengthen you in those areas. If you believe we are made in God's image, then you know He can turn your feelings about who you are around.

BOOK TABLE OF CONTENTS

Pt. 1   UNDERSTANDING SELF-ESTEEM
   Unit 1   What is Self-Esteem?
   Unit 2   The Rise and Fall of Self-Esteem
   Unit 3   Where Does Self-Esteem Come From?

Pt. 2   THE CAUSES OF LOW-ESTEEM
   Unit 4   Negative Thinking
   Unit 5   Mistaken Beliefs
   Unit 6   Comparisons and Your Self-Esteem
   Unit 7   Perfectionism

Pt. 3   BUILD YOUR SELF-ESTEEM
   Unit 8   Know Thyself
   Unit 9   Express Yourself
   Unit 10 Know Your Values
   Unit 11 Positive Self-Talk
   Unit 12 I Like Myself!

Barbara J. Braham & Merle Wood, Self-Esteem and Getting Ahead (South-Western's Life Series), South-Western Pub (May 1992)

IF I CAN'T BE THE CAKE, I WON'T BE THE CRUMZ

WHY ARE RELATIONSHIPS "HARD"

4. DO YOU REALLY "HEAR" ME?

In order for a Christians to trust God with how they relate and respond when others offend them, they have to trust Him with everything in their lives. When you don't trust and believe God will do what he says He will, you find it hard to hear the voice of the Holy Spirit when He guides, leads, and directs you. For most non-believers, when a voice speaks to them out the blue, they refer to it by saying "something told me that", or "my sixth sense told me", but when you have a relationship with the Lord, you respect that voice as the Holy Spirit trying to guide you. A key factor in establishing trust and faith in the Lord's direction is for you to believe and accept that God is the sovereign ruler of the Universe *(Psalm 103:19)*,

ORIGINAL

YOUNG GIRL

OLD LADY

and you have faith that God will do what He says He will do *(Hebrews 11:6)* in ALL things including your relationships with others. It's easy to believe God with simple matters, but when people in your life hurt or wrong you, many times you want to respond like Madea. You want them "got" right then and there, and not later. When you're hurt, it seem like God is taking too long to right your wrong, however, His timing and your timing are not the same. When someone hurts you, you have to learn how to stop taking what seems like attacks "personally". You have to look deeper into the issue and not only process what they ARE SAYING, by learning how to discern WHAT THEY ARE NOT SAYING. What is the "hidden" message in what they are telling you? For instance, if you only looked at the first picture on the left and I told you there were two women in the picture, do you see them?

The art of EFFECTIVE COMMUNICATION with others is learning how to "hear" when someone tries to get you to see their view especially when your view is different than theirs. Do you try to see the other person's point of view or perspective or are you stuck in your own perception about what you think it is, or it should be? Just like these pictures, your brain is conditioned to see life through filters. Your filters are your views about the world which are impacted and distorted by the filters created during your childhood, by your life models, society's views, and your experiences. When you stop trying to make people only see your viewpoint, and you slow down and try to hear theirs, you start showing empathy and respect to others which is very important in establishing and maintaining healthy relationships.

IF I CAN'T BE THE CAKE, I WON'T BE THE CRUMZ

5. COMMUNICATION, COMMUNICATION, COMMUNICATION

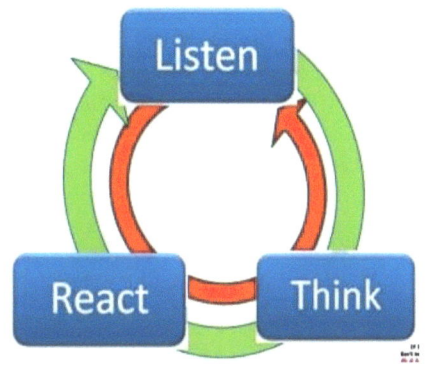

If you want to see a change in others, you must first start with "yourself." Many times the message you are trying to convey with others might not be received or heard by them the way you expected it to. The art of effective communication is not on the receiver but on you the sender of the message. If a person does not respond to your message the way you expect them too, that is because they did not understand or hear it the way you wanted them too. Communication is not just about what is said, it is how it is said, the words that are used, and many times your body language when you are saying it. There is a science and an art to effective communication. The first task is to understand how you are communicating to others. Then once you understand your form of communication, you need to evaluate how others communicate their message to you. Women are not taught how to communicate effectively so they "assume" others will automatically understand them; when in fact the problem is how ineffective their form of communication is. In order to truly communicate effectively with others; you must first understand your needs, wants, and desires. Once you have figured out what you need, then you can take time to get to know what others need. Then as you are listening to what they are sharing, the art of understanding the message is learning how to Hear them, and what they are trying to say to you, without your trying to get your point of view across first. "Listening" without "Hearing" is just noise. In other words, if someone is talking to you, and you are not paying attention to what they are saying, then you are just listening to noise until it is your time to talk. The next time you are trying to get your point across to someone, try to do the following communication techniques;

1) Tell them what you want them to know
2) When they don't respond in the way you thought they would have, don't take it personally, just regroup and possibly restate the message
3) If they don't understand you the next time, then you can try to restate it again
4) If they don't understand again, then you both might need to agree to disagree or to table the conversation for a later date/time

Don't be upset and react when you are frustrated. Stay calm, be patient, and ask yourself WHY AM I UPSET? Getting a resolution to that question and not your emotions is the most effective form of resolving communication challenges.

WHY ARE RELATIONSHIPS "HARD"

6. THE FROG IN THE POT ANALOGY

A frog in a swamp is in it's natural environment even when the temperature of the water in the swamp is over 100 degrees, the frog is comfortable because he is used to that climate. If you take that same frog and put it in a pot of cold water on a stove, the frog remains in the pot because it is still in it's natural element of water. If you turn the heat on the stove up incrementally, from one, to two, to three, then to four or five, the frog still remains in the pot because the water isn't too hot, or too cold. It is still a "comfortable" environment to him. But when you start to turn the stove up to six and seven, the water starts getting warmer and the frog still remains in the pot because he starts ADJUSTING! He adjusts at six, then at seven, then at eight, until you keep turning the heat up on the stove incrementally all the way to ten when you find yourself with FROG SOUP. The analogy of the frog in a pot is likened to how we deal with the issues in our lives because many times you find yourself adjusting to situations where it seems you should be asking yourself "Why am I still here?" When you suppress your emotions and frustrations, overtime you start feeling overwhelmed like the problems in your life are too complicated to solve and fix. The reason you feel this way is because you have not been told or been given the okay to put your needs first or to advocate for what you want and need. Life is about balance and it is not good to suppress your feelings and let things build up into a massive ball of emotions and problems.

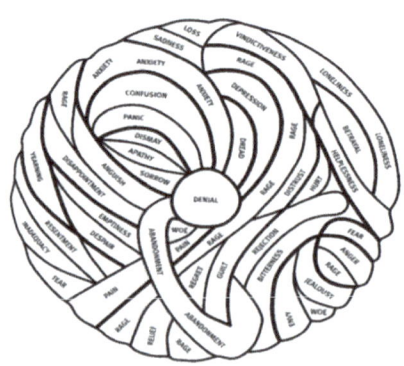

IF I CAN'T BE THE CAKE, I WON'T BE THE CRUMZ

7. POWER & CONTROL

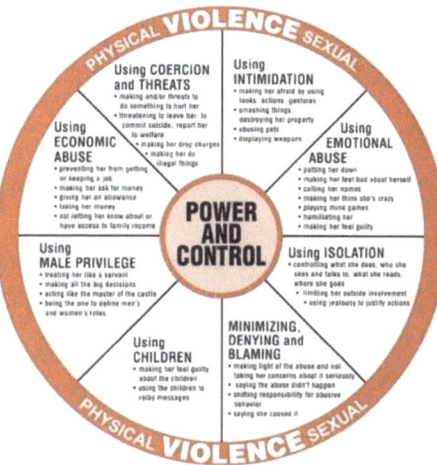

Another challenge that exists in relationships today is our blinded need to get the person we care about to exhibit behavior we feel is "better" for them. Or we desire for them to stop doing the things they are doing because we feel it is hurting them or our relationship with them. When you find yourself constantly telling the people you care about and especially those you love about their "imperfections" or how great their life would be if they took your advice because you know what's best for them, you are actually trying to "CONTROL" them. When it seems as if you have tried everything in your power to get them to change, and they won't listen or change their ways, you start thinking of different things to say or do to get them to do what you want them to do. Over time, you start exhibiting some of the actions outlined on this POWER AND CONTROL WHEEL. When you use psychological, emotional, behavioral, physical, and sexual tactics to get them to give you what you want, that is the behavior defined as "Control". Even though most people understand the reality that people don't have to do what you want them too, when you really want them to change, you tend to forget that fact. People who use tactics identified in the Power Wheel don't realize they are actually MANIPULATORS, USERS, AND ABUSERS. Many times, the behavior is not "intentional" because as a child they watched the people in their lives like their parents and family members treat others that way so it became acceptable learned behavior. Whether it is intentional or not, you have to see the signs, and ask yourself if you really want to be with someone who does not appreciate you for the person you are. Offering constructive criticism is human nature, but when advice or opinions turn in to life-altering expectations, their constant need to critique, criticize, demean, and "improve" you no longer feels like love. It starts to feel as if you are living in a prison. The only person who has the power to change your willingness to be controlled by others is YOU. Because women are nurturers and caretakers, women feel with their hearts first before they think with their heads, so people who do not have the best intentions will use your desire to help others into a weapon against you.

REFLECTION

Do you practice walking in someone else's shoes or try adopting a new perspective as a great way of solving communication issues with others? Do your try to ask yourself "What would so and so do here?"or, "What would they say about this situation?" By looking at the conflict you have experienced in your relationships with others, you gain a greater perspective about your issues with them, and you learn about their issues with you. Reflecting on the both parties concerns about the issues in the relationship will help you to be more empathetic with others so that you can see all sides of the story and not just your view. This helps you become more objective and thereby create a win-win outcome for the situation.

So how about you walk in other people's shoes for a bit? Your colleagues', loved ones, and your friends to see what you notice when you step outside your own world-view or way of thinking. Try to "hear" what they are saying and not just "listen" to them. Don't try to change their mind, work harder to understand their point of view!

REFLECTION EXERCISES

As you review the scriptures outlined here, think about the things you need to KEEP DOING, START DOING, and STOP DOING that will help you identify healthier, loving, boundaries for yourself and with others. Stop looking for people to FIGURE YOU OUT! Identify your 80/20 and start living your life assessing the things that will help you be a better you.

REFLECTION SCRIPTURES

BOOK	SCRIPTURE
Roman 12:3	When you are Prideful
Luke 18:1-8	Why you doubt God wants to hear from you
Col 3:13	When someone has wronged you
1 Peter 5:7	When you are anxious
Ps 102	When you feel sorry for yourself
Peter 14:30	When you are jealous of others success
Eph 3:20	When you doubt that God is able
Matthew 11:28-30	When you carry a heavy load
Psalm 25:9	When you need direction
Psalm 42:5	When you are blue

Why are relationships "hard"

MY 80/20 CHECKLIST

- ☐ I need to get a better understanding about healthy relationships
- ☐ Today going forward I am committed to identifying my 80/20
- ☐ I can't change the past, but I can change my future
- ☐ I won't blame others for what they do to me
- ☐ However, I recognize I must advocate for my happiness and
- ☐ Set boundaries for those who inadvertently hurt me physically, emotionally, and psychologically

OTHER NOTES

_____
_____
_____
_____
_____
_____
_____
_____
_____
_____
_____
_____
_____
_____
_____
_____

IF I CAN'T BE THE CAKE, I WON'T BE THE CRUMZ

WHY ARE RELATIONSHIPS "HARD"

THINGS TO KEEP DOING

_____
_____
_____
_____
_____
_____
_____
_____

THINGS TO START DOING

_____
_____
_____
_____
_____
_____
_____
_____

THINGS TO STOP DOING

_____
_____
_____
_____
_____
_____
_____
_____

IF I CAN'T BE THE CAKE, I WON'T BE THE CRUMZ

RELATIONSHIPS ARE HARD

Each day that I awake,
it's to the loneliness that's buried so deep within

Seeking, searching,
soul mate or just a forever friend.

Somebody to share those lonely moments
and heartfelt thoughts with

Trying to forget yesterday pain of them,
with not having guilt.

I'm guilty of not loving me for all my many
accomplishments that I made

I'm guilty of giving my heart to so many takers,
like I was getting paid.

I long to share that space with that someone
and in hope that it's you

Counting the tick -tocks on the clock,
time running out;
wanting a oneness that is true.

But I realize one thing relationships are hard,
and people are too.

By Riah (2017)

What Do You Need To Be Happy

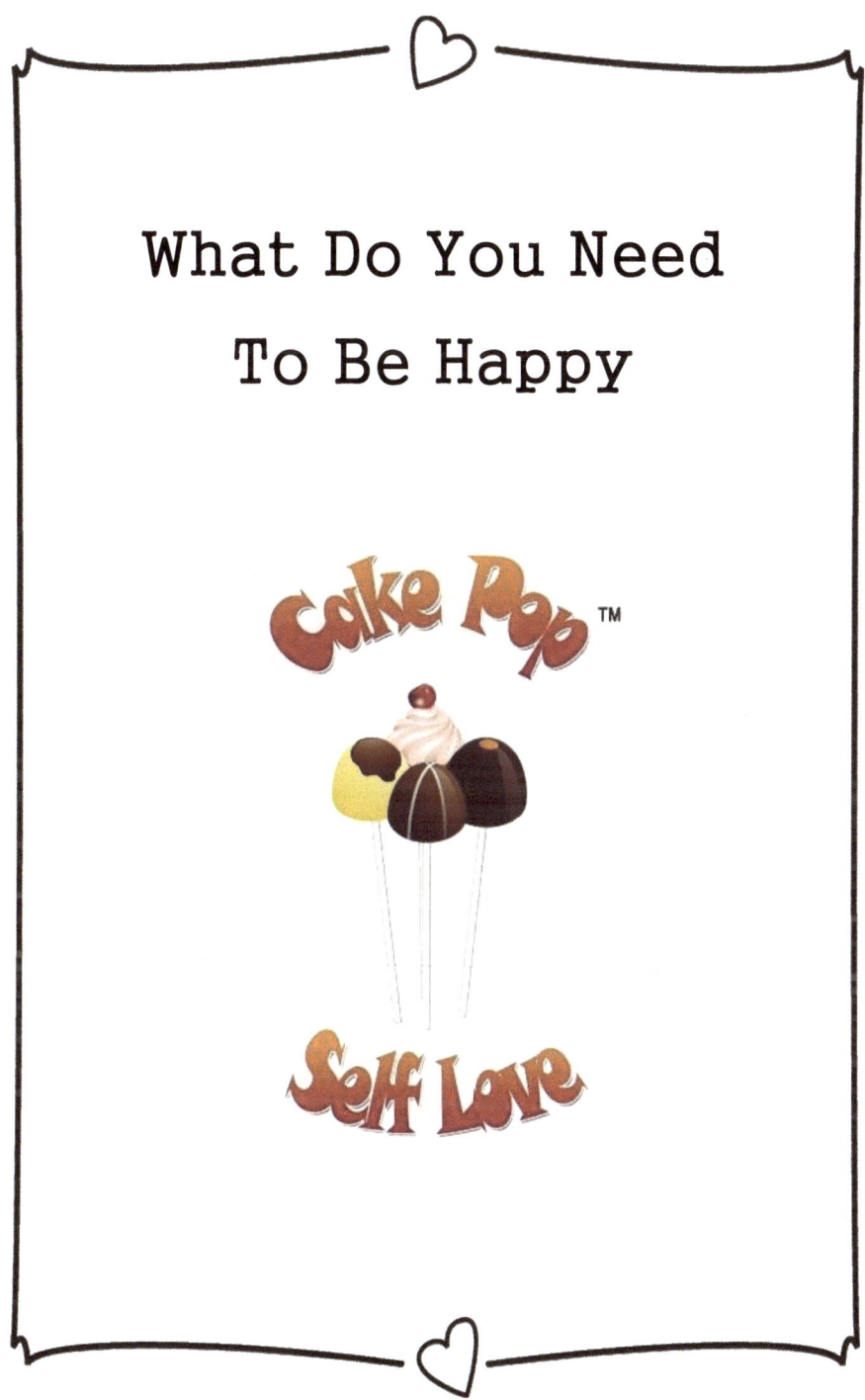

CAKE POP - SELF LOVE

WHAT DO YOU NEED TO BE HAPPY
WHAT IS YOUR 80/20?

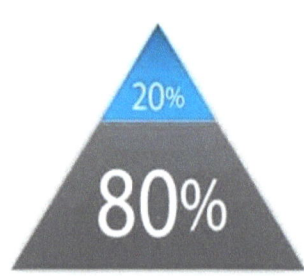

In a dysfunctional household someone tends to cause everyone else in the house to focus on "that person's issue" or "that person's needs" to the point where you grow up taking care of, or worrying more about others than yourself. Living in a household where your opinion or views don't feel like they matter cause you to become an adult living with the acceptance of "lies" from others than to stand on a foundation of truth. Most of us either grew up in a "dysfunctional" household or are currently living in one. Before you can ever make someone else happy, you first have to get in touch with your EMOTIONAL, PSYCHOLOGICAL, and BEHAVIORAL needs. Until you can identify what you need to be happy, you won't know if the people in your life are genuinely for you or against you. The Cake Chronicles 80/20 Healthy Relationship Challenge encourages you to do just that. In order to know if you have the right people in your life, you have to define what happiness means to you. This is your 80%. How can you ever know if the people in your life are **FOR YOU** or **AGAINST YOU** if you really don't know what you need? Your 80% includes thoughts and consideration about the following topics;

1) What your goals are,
2) Your joys,
3) Your sorrows,
4) Your fears,
5) Your problems,
6) Your communication techniques,
7) Your desires or motivations,
8) Your feelings,
9) Your spiritual gifts,
10) Your temptations to sin, and your
11) Boundaries.

Once you have identified your 80%, you have to determine what you are willing to compromise or your 20%. Because no one is PERFECT, you have to know the behaviors you can accept, tolerate, or need to compromise. That is your 20% or the MAXIMUM differences you will accept. You should never compromise more than 20%, because you will start feeling CRUMZY, unhappy, frustrated, and miserable.

IF I CAN'T BE THE CAKE, I WON'T BE THE CRUMZ

1. AVOID "ICING" TYPE RELATIONSHIPS

The first step in getting someone else to know and love you, is to

1) Know yourself and then
2) Love the woman God made you to be.

Many times women are told to love the woman God made them to be. However, they are not taught how to do that! Without identifying your gifts as well as your flaws, women struggle establishing healthy relationships with people who are truly made by God to be in their lives. They date Mr. Zero because they overlook Mr. Hero. Teddy Pendergrass had a song titled *"I Can't Help Nobody Until I Help Myself."* You can't love anyone until you know how to love yourself. Until you understand the science of self-esteem and the components of loving yourself, you will find it hard appreciating the people who genuinely want to be in your life because you are accepting the people you should keep at a distance.

In 1998, Prophetess Juanita Bynum profoundly shared in her relationship series titled *"No More Sheets,"* how as a single woman she struggled with discerning if a man she met was the guy God had for her. Many times women get so caught up in how good he looks on "paper", his appearance, and the materialistic gains from the relationship, they don't take the time that is needed to see what his values, morals, and ethics are. The Cake Chronicles philosophy of judging a book by it's cover is called ICING. They might look good, they might taste good, but they are not good for you! Steve Harvey shared in his book *"Act Like A Lady, Think Like A Man"* that a woman needs to wait at least 90 days to see where the relationships is going. This 90-day rule is profound for single women interested in dating because at a minimum it can take that long for a person's "true" self to appear. It's easy to fall in love with him during the FIRST MONTH SUGAR phase, but you need those 90 days to see if you need to FIGHT OR FLIGHT!

CAKE POP - SELF LOVE

2. GETTING YOUR EMOTIONAL NEEDS MET

Today we are living in a time where people care more about how they feel, than the reality of the situation. There is nothing wrong with being in touch with your emotions. The challenge is ensuring you don't let your emotions govern your thoughts, views, and decisions. Another ingredient in the 80/20 process is determining the things that bring you joy or happiness. In this first exercise, get in touch with your EMOTIONAL NEEDS by identifying below all of the things that make YOUR HEART SING! If money was not an option or issue, what are the things that are important to you, physically, emotionally, spiritually, and even materialistically? Your 80% begins with you asking yourself this question.

WHAT MAKES YOUR HEART SING?

1. _____
2. _____
3. _____
4. _____
5. _____
6. _____
7. _____
8. _____
9. _____
10. _____
11. _____
12. _____
13. _____
14. _____
15. _____
16. _____
17. _____
18. _____

IF I CAN'T BE THE CAKE, I WON'T BE THE CRUMZ

3. YOUR LIFE MAP

In order to be free to live your best life now, you have to take a look back over your life to reflect on your past so that it can no longer impact your future. In this exercise, you will draw a life map.

1. On a blank piece of paper turned horizontally, draw a line from left to right.
2. Record your birth on the left-edge of the paper.
3. Draw a line in the middle to represent half your age.
4. And the right edge represents today.
5. Map the high points with peaks and the low points with valleys.
6. With each mark, write your age and a description what the peaks & troughs represent (e.g. moved to a new city, university, graduated, or parents divorced etc).
8. Before answering the review questions below ask yourself, "What are the small and big events that stand out to me about my life?" Add them to your map?
9. Here are some questions to think about before you get started:
    - What are the significant milestones/events in your life to date?
    - What things have you done that you're proud of? (Achievements big and small, from childhood onwards)
    - What were you interested in as a child? What were your childhood passions?

LIFE MAP EXAMPLE:

This exercise is meant to be completed quickly – just turn over, start drawing the line and see where it takes you. Don't over think the events you put on the timeline Just note what comes to mind. Once you're done, review the events in your life that stand out to you in an effort of understanding what events in your life have shaped, and contributed to you becoming the unique person you are today!

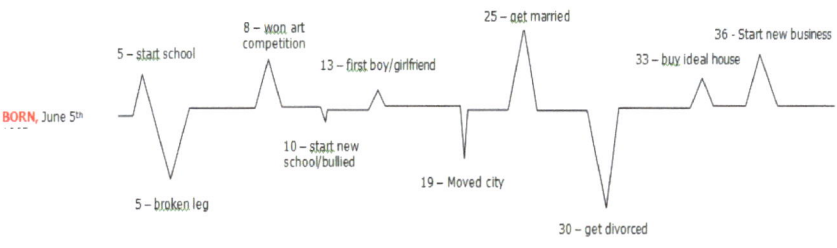

IF I CAN'T BE THE CAKE, I WON'T BE THE CRUMZ

4. WHAT IS YOUR DEFINITION OF LOVE?

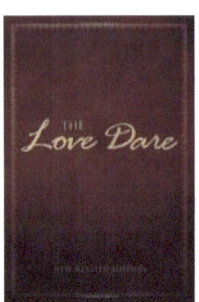

When someone tells you they love you or when you say you love them, what do you really mean? Love should be defined and in order for you to know if you truly love someone, or if they love you the way you need to be loved, their behavior should include characteristics that match your expectations. I realized this concept when I watched the movie *"Fireproof"* and ordered the book the *"The Love Dare"* which was based on the principles outlined in the movie. Many times people get into a relationship not knowing what their definition of love really is. Check all of the characteristics that are important in your definition of LOVE! YES means you need that characteristic and it is in your definition of love. NO means this is not required. Make sure the behavior of the people who say they "love you" model your expectation for love, keeping in mind that their definition of love might be different than yours. When someone does not treat you how you want to be treated, you can't help them understand what needs to change if you can't define it. The list below is not an exhaustive list, but it is a great start to help you begin the process of defining what loving you entails and should really look like.

YES	NO		YES	NO	
		Love is Patient			Love promotes intimacy
		Love is Kind			Love seeks to understand
		Love is Thoughtful			Love is possible
		Love is NOT rude			Love is faithful
		Love is NOT irritable			Love always protects
		Love believes the best			Love vs Lust
		Love is NOT jealous			Love forgives
		Loves makes good impressions			Love is responsible
		Love is unconditional			Love encourages
		Love cherishes			Love makes sacrifices
		Love let's the other win			Love is accountable
		Love fights fair			Love completes each other
		Love takes delight			Love fulfills dreams
		Love is honorable			Love endures
		Love is a covenant			

Alex Kendrick and Stephen Kendrick, The Love Dare, B&H Books; Revised edition (2013)

5. ESTABLISHING BOUNDARIES AND BALANCE

Something else that is difficult for women to do is to say NO and establish "healthy" boundaries. Learning how to establish healthy boundaries is key in order for you to stop "settling" for less than God wants for you. According to Wikipedia, *"A boundary is defined as a line, point, or plane that indicates or fixes a limit or extent."* Boundaries are also limits we set in relationships that allow us to protect ourselves from being hurt, frustrated, or let down. A firm boundary lets those around you know what you find acceptable or not acceptable. Boundaries come from having a good sense of self-worth. Boundaries make it possible for you to separate your own thoughts and feelings from the views, thoughts, and opinions of others, and help you take responsibility for what you think, feel and do. Boundaries allow you to rejoice in your own uniqueness. Intact boundaries are flexible, so they allow you to get close to others. Good boundaries protect you from abuse, help you to take care of yourself, and at times, allow you to distinguish your limitations. Everyone has the right to set boundaries in various aspects of their lives.

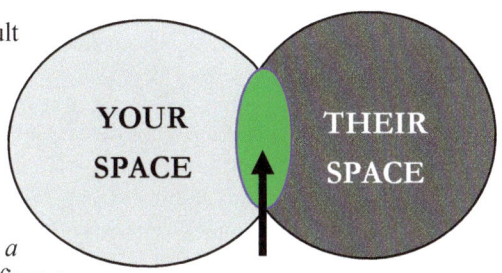

The BOUNDARY

There's an old saying *"Fool me once, shame on you. Fool me twice, shame on me."* If love doesn't hurt, and you find yourself being hurt by your loved ones, ask yourself what are they doing that upsets you. Your hurt feelings and emotions are actually triggers to tell you that something is being said or done that frighten you or remind you of something that bothers you. The issue is not that they "purposely" tried to hurt you; it's trying to figure out why it bothered you. If you have never thought about defining boundaries, you will continue feeling CRUMZY because you have not identified your 20%. The following are types of personal areas where you need to define boundaries:

⇒ Intellectual/Mental Boundaries

⇒ Physical Boundaries

⇒ Emotional Boundaries

6. WHAT IS YOUR LOVE LANGUAGE?

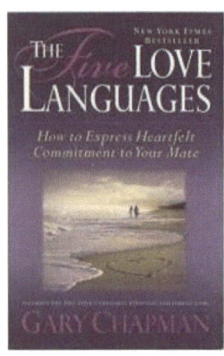

According to Dr. Gary Chapman, when a person's primary love language is being met, they feel loved and appreciated. Your love language is how you express love, or want to receive love from others. But if your primary language is not being met, then you feel empty and unloved. It is important for you to understand your primary love language because this will help you determine if the person in your life is capable of loving you the way you need to be loved. Once you determine your language, share it with the important people in your life. If they are willing to show you love in the manner that is important to you, then you can see that they care for you. The love languages are a part of your 80/20 and are identified as;

1) Acts of Service - Feel loved when someone does something for you (cleans their room, or washes the dishes)

2) Quality Time - Feel loved when someone spends time with you (going for walks, watching TV, going to the movies, and taking trips)

3) Physical Touch - Feel loved when you physically are close to people (hugs, embraces, intimacy, you know, touchy-feely people)

4) Gifts - Feel loved when someone buys you things or you enjoy giving things to people

5) and Words of Affirmation - Feel loved when someone gives you compliments or you love giving people compliments.

I believe people who cheat do so because their primary love language of "Physical Touch" is so strong, they don't realize that not being physical with their partner, (holding hands, embracing, hugging, and intimacy) causes them to yearn to be close to someone. If their partner is not aware of their strong need to be close, then their absence or distance will cause an issue for their partner. It is possible for you to have more than one primary language. But not knowing your language or your mates can be the death of your relationship. Purchase the book, or take the online assessments to learn your Love Language (s).

Dr. Gary Chapman, The 5 Love Languages: The Secret to Love That Lasts by Chapman, Gary D Published by Northfield Publishing New edition (2009) Paperback, Northfield Publishing,2009

7. UNHEALTHY COMMUNICATION STYLES

It is difficult establishing "healthy" relationships if you communicate in a way that hide your true feelings. When you don't really like yourself, you try to "pretend" that you do, and the way you pretend is called *"The Mask You Wear."* Trying to be something that you're not, or acting as if everything is okay when it really isn't only hurts you, and not the people you are lying, and pretending with. This is also a way to self-sabotage your hopes and dreams which in turn cause you to believe you are not trustworthy or worthy of receiving all that God has for you. Search online for the phrases below, or read about them in the self-esteem book identified on page 29.

	UNHEALTHY COMMUNICA-TION STYLES	I AM LIKE THIS TYPE		UNHEALTHY COMMUNICA-TION STYLES	I AM LIKE THIS TYPE
1	Busybody		10	Volcano	
2	Antagonist		11	Sherman Tank	
3	Indecisive		12	Space Cadet	
4	Complainer		13	Crybaby	
5	Spoiler		14	Garbage Collector	
6	Dead Beat		15	User	
7	Know-It-All		16	Macho/Tough Mask	
8	Mr. Nice Guy		17	I'm the Greatest	
9	Ms. Nice Gal		18	Blaming and Complaining Mask	

IF I CAN'T BE THE CAKE, I WON'T BE THE CRUMZ

8. CODEPENDENT TENDENCIES

Women naturally are "nurturers". They have a tendency to help and take care of people and their problems. Women are rarely taught that sometimes their desire to help can in fact "hurt" them. Purchase the book *"Codependent No More"* by Melody Beattie and discover the true understanding about co-dependent behavior. You can also search online for the terms below to see if you have an unhealthy habit of neglecting yourself because you are always taking care of other people's problems. There is nothing wrong with helping, but when helping becomes hurtful to the person you are trying to help or even to yourself, you have to evaluate your behavior so tyou can understand how to establish healthy boundaries to learn when enough is really enough.

	CO-DEPENDENT/CARETAKER TENDENCY	**I EXEMPLIFY THIS TYPE**
1	Low Self Worth	
2	Repression	
3	Obsession	
4	Denial	
5	Weak Boundaries	
6	Dependency	
7	Lack of Trust	
8	Anger	
9	Intimacy Problems	
10	Progressive	
11	Other Unhealthy Behaviors	

Melody Beattie, Codependent No More: How to Stop Controlling Others and Start Caring for Yourself, Hazelden; 1st edition (1986)

9. WORDS NOT TO SAY

There is power in the words and phrases we use with others. Be mindful of hurtful words, phrases and tones taken when you are speaking with others. Hurt people Hurt people and when you use hurtful words, you innately wound those you care about. In the book *"Imperfect Phrases for Relationships,"* Robert Bacal identifies over 100+ hurtful phrases people use every day that can cause others to be "defensive" of you. Purchase the book to see how many of those phrases you use on a daily basis. Before you can establish healthy communication patterns with others you have to do your part to ensure you are not wounding them.

- ☐ Just Leave It, I'll Do It Myself (a destructive phrase with children).
- ☐ It's No Big Deal
- ☐ Lighten Up
- ☐ Listen To Yourself
- ☐ Most People Do It
- ☐ Never Mind
- ☐ No Problem, I'm Used To Being Dumped On
- ☐ No I don't/yes you do - Pointless Ego Arguments
- ☐ How To Say No Without Making Them Mad
- ☐ Stop Lecturing and Being Patronizing: Why You Shouldn't Say: Nobody Said Life Is Fair
- ☐ Not Now
- ☐ Nothing Is The Matter
- ☐ Nothing I Do Is Ever Good Enough
- ☐ Pull Yourself Together
- ☐ "Relax"
- ☐ "Should I Repeat This For the Fourth Time"
- ☐ "Snap Out of It"
- ☐ "Sorry But..."
- ☐ Stop Being So Emotional
- ☐ "Take It Or Leave It"
- ☐ "That Doesn't Make Any Sense"
- ☐ Stop Being Insensitive
- ☐ "What Until Your Father Gets Home".
- ☐ If Only You...
- ☐ We Have To Talk
- ☐ "Whatever"
- ☐ What Do You Want ME To Do About It,
- ☐ It's not MY problem
- ☐ "What's Wrong With You?" Hides a Judgment In A Question
- ☐ "When Will You Start...Looking for A Job?" or other similar phrases
- ☐ "Who Do You Think You Are?"
- ☐ Why Can't You Be More Like...?
- ☐ Why Don't You Talk To Me?
- ☐ Why Do You Need To Know?
- ☐ Why Is It Always Me That?
- ☐ Why Is This Such A Big Deal To You?
- ☐ Why Should I Care?
- ☐ Why Should I Apologize...I Didn't Do Anything
- ☐ Why Would I Be Upset...Just Because...
- ☐ Will You Be On Time THIS Time?
- ☐ You Always...
- ☐ You Aren't Listening
- ☐ You Can't...
- ☐ You Don't Appreciate...
- ☐ You Don't Know What You Are Talking About
- ☐ You Drink Too Much
- ☐ You Knew I Was This Way When You Married Me
- ☐ You Made Me Do It
- ☐ You Make Me Feel Stupid
- ☐ You Never Asked
- ☐ You Never
- ☐ You Should Talk. You're Worse Than I AM
- ☐ You Shouldn't Feel That Way
- ☐ You Started It
- ☐ You Take Everything Too Seriously
- ☐ You Tell Me
- ☐ You'll Be OK. Don't Worry About It
- ☐ You're Disrespecting Me
- ☐ You Aren't Being Logical
- ☐ You're Just Like...
- ☐ You're Over Reacting
- ☐ You're The Only One That Thinks That...

Robert Bacal, Imperfect Phrases For Relationships: 101 COMMON Things You Should Never Say To Someone Important To You... And What To Say Instead (ImPerfect Phrases Series), Bacal & Associates (March 11, 2012)

10. ARE YOU PASSIVE OR AGGRESSIVE?

It is difficult establishing "healthy" relationships if you communicate in either a passive or an aggressive manner. People who are passive have a hard time expressing themselves so they tend to avoid "conflicts" and "confrontation". Aggressive people tend to dominate over others and disregard other's feelings or views. The challenge with these two types of communication styles is they are ineffective forms of communicating with others. Many times, if you find yourself alone and lonely, just maybe you are driving people away because of how you communicate with them. It is easy to see how someone has offended you, but have you ever evaluated how you may have offended them.

	CRAYZMAKER TENDENCIES	I EXIBIT THIS TYPE
1	The Avoider	
2	The Pseudo Accommodator	
3	The Guilt Maker	
4	The Subject Changer	
5	The Distracter	
6	The Mind Reader	
7	The Trapper	
8	The Crisis Ticker	
9	The Gunny Sacker	
10	The Trivial Tyrannizer	
11	The Belt Liner	
12	The Joker	
13	The Blamer	
14	The Contract Tyrannizer	
15	The Kitchen Sink Fighter	
16	The Withholder	
17	The Benedict Arnold	

11. UNDERSTANDING YOUR FEELINGS & EMOTIONS

Your "NEEDS" are basic personal, emotional, and psychological requirements that must be fulfilled in order for you to feel safe, secure and complete. If your needs are not met, then you find yourself feeling unsatisfied and do everything you can to get others to meet your needs either directly or indirectly. When you identify your 80/20, you become an advocate for yourself because you know what you need to be happy and you realize the ownership to advocate for what you need is YOU! You can't help others understand what you need and want if you don't have a clear idea about it yourself.

Emotions are God given triggers when we are happy or sad. Positive emotions confirm that our needs are being met. Negative emotions are triggers that cause you to feel afraid or upset which in turn cause you to feel unhappy. Using the list below, identify the positive and negative emotions have you experienced over the last year. After you review the list, if you find more red emotions than green, then you have been very overwhelmed with unhealthy negative emotions. When someone triggers a red emotion, you need to STOP and ask yourself why does their behavior trigger this negative emotion? Until you get an understanding of why the behavior bothers you, will continue to feel that way and to respond and feel drained by these negative emotions.

HEALTHY/HAPPY EMOTIONS

AFFECTIONATE	EXHILIRATED
Sympathetic	Ecstatic
Compassionate	Elated
Friendly	Thrilled
Loving	**GRATEFUL**
Open Hearted	Appreciative
CONFIDENT	Moved
Empowered	Thankful
Open	**HOPEFUL**
Safe	Expectant
ENGAGED	Encouraged
Alert	Optimistic
Curious	**JOYFUL**
Fascinated	Delighted
Interested	Happy
Intrigued	Pleased
Stimulated	**PEACEFUL**
INSPIRED	Calm
Amazed	Clear Headed
Awed	Content
Wonder	Fulfilled
EXCITED	Relaxed
Animated	Satisfied
Astonished	Trusting
Energetic	**REFRESHED**
Enthusiastic	Rejuvenated
Giddy	Renewed
Invigorated	Rested
Lively	Restored
Passionate	Revived

UNHEALTHY/SAD EMOTIONS

AFRAID	AVERSION	DISQUIET	SAD
Apprehensive	Animosity	Agitated	Depressed
Dread	Appalled	Disturbed	Disappointed
Frightened	Disgusted	Perturbed	Discouraged
Mistrustful	Dislike	Restless	Hopeless
Panicked	Hate	Shocked	Unhappy
Petrified	Horrified	Surprised	**TENSE**
Scared	Hostile	Troubled	Cranky
Suspicious	Repulsed	Uncomfortable	Edgy
Terrified	**CONFUSED**	Uneasy	Fidgety
Worried	Baffled	Unsettled	Irritable
ANNOYED	Bewildered	Upset	Nervous
Aggravated	Hesitant	**EMBARRASSED**	Overwhelmed
Dismayed	Lost	Ashamed	Restless
Disgruntled	Perplexed	Guilty	Stressed out
Displeased	Puzzled	Mortified	**VULNERABLE**
Frustrated	Torn	Self-conscious	Fragile
Impatient	**DISCONNECTED**	**FATIGUE**	Helpless
Irritated	Alienated	Beat	Insecure
Irked	Bored	Depleted	Reserved
ANGRY	Cold	Exhausted	Sensitive
Enraged	Distant	Sleepy	**YEARNING**
Furious	Distracted	Tired	Envious
Indignant	Uninterested	Worn out	Jealous
Irate	Withdrawn	**PAIN**	Longing
Livid		Agony	Pining
Outraged		Anguished	
Resentful		Bereaved	
		Devastated	
		Heartbroken	
		Hurt	
		Lonely	
		Miserable	
		Regretful	

IF I CAN'T BE THE CAKE, I WON'T BE THE CRUMZ

CAKE POP - SELF LOVE

REFLECTION SCRIPTURES

BOOK	SCRIPTURE
Psalm 37:23-24	When you fear failure
Psalm 139:13-18	When you doubt your worth
Ephesians 4:26-27	When you are angry
Roman 5:1-5	When you don't feel at peace with God
Proverbs 11:9	With their words, the godless destroy their friends

OlSelf Love

One day you will realize you are enough.
You won't have to internalize everything that goes wrong,
thinking there is something wrong with you.
You will look in the mirror & love what you see.
You will be so absorbed in yourself that what others think will not matter.
You will be happy.
You will be grateful for the experiences that got you where you needed to be.
You will not seek validation from anyone, but yourself.
You will be genuine to those around you regardless of those who are not.
You will take the time to grow, even if it's through concrete.
You will water yourself.
You will reek of happiness, that can not be taking away.
You will find serenity.
You will be mindful of who you let in, but will not walk on eggshells
blocking blessings.
You will know what is for you & what is not…& you will accept that.
You will cry only tears of joy.
You will not over think every situation, instead let it flow.
You will live your life to its full potential, not holding back.
You will rise above.
You will live.
You will be great.
One day you will realize that you are enough.

Mariah James (2017)

IF I CAN'T BE THE CAKE, I WON'T BE THE CRUMZ

PERSONAL REFLECTIONS FROM CLIENTS

The Cake Chronicles' philosophy was not developed overnight. As a young single mother striving to maintain healthy relationships, the concepts identified in this book were derived from my personal life experiences, and my meditations with God where I asked Him to help me understand what was wrong not only in my relationships with others, but the dynamics of all types of unhealthy relationships. In 2017 while conducting a seminar, I asked the participants to provide feedback about the Cake Chronicles 80/20 Healthy Relationship Challenge. At the back of each section in this book are the actual "personal" reflections noted by participants from the seminars. Review their reflections, then on the pages identified, note what you will KEEP, START, and STOP doing to be a healthier, happier you!

I should pay more attention to my 80%

♡

This philosophy is taken from the word of God!

♡

Start using my relationship with God and apply His teachings to my life

♡

Really try and define what will make me happy

♡

The homework from the lessons showed me I need to do some work

REFLECTIONS FROM CLIENTS

Learning about Love Languages

♡

Being more honest with my feelings

♡

Watch the words I say

♡

Learn to be more patient

♡

Continue working on "not thinking about me" and work on defining balance in my life

♡

Learning to look in the mirror

♡

Move your boyfriend out of your Husband way. I struggle with worldly things in my relationships because of the way I communicate with others

♡

To Know Yourself

♡

I plan to do a 360 in every area

♡

How to react when I'm triggered

CAKE POP - SELF LOVE

MY 80/20 CAKE POP CHECKLIST

- [ ] I WILL take the time to define my 80/20
- [ ] I will not settle for less than my 80/20 now that I know what it is
- [ ] I understand I only have the power to change ME
- [ ] I know I am wonderfully and beautifully made
- [ ] When I am triggered, I will think before I react

OTHER NOTES

_____
_____
_____
_____
_____
_____
_____
_____
_____
_____
_____
_____
_____
_____
_____
_____
_____
_____
_____
_____
_____

IF I CAN'T BE THE CAKE, I WON'T BE THE CRUMZ

CAKE POP - SELF LOVE

THINGS TO KEEP DOING

_____
_____
_____
_____
_____
_____
_____
_____

THINGS TO START DOING

_____
_____
_____
_____
_____
_____
_____
_____

THINGS TO STOP DOING

_____
_____
_____
_____
_____
_____
_____
_____

IF I CAN'T BE THE CAKE, I WON'T BE THE CRUMZ

Relationships with Others

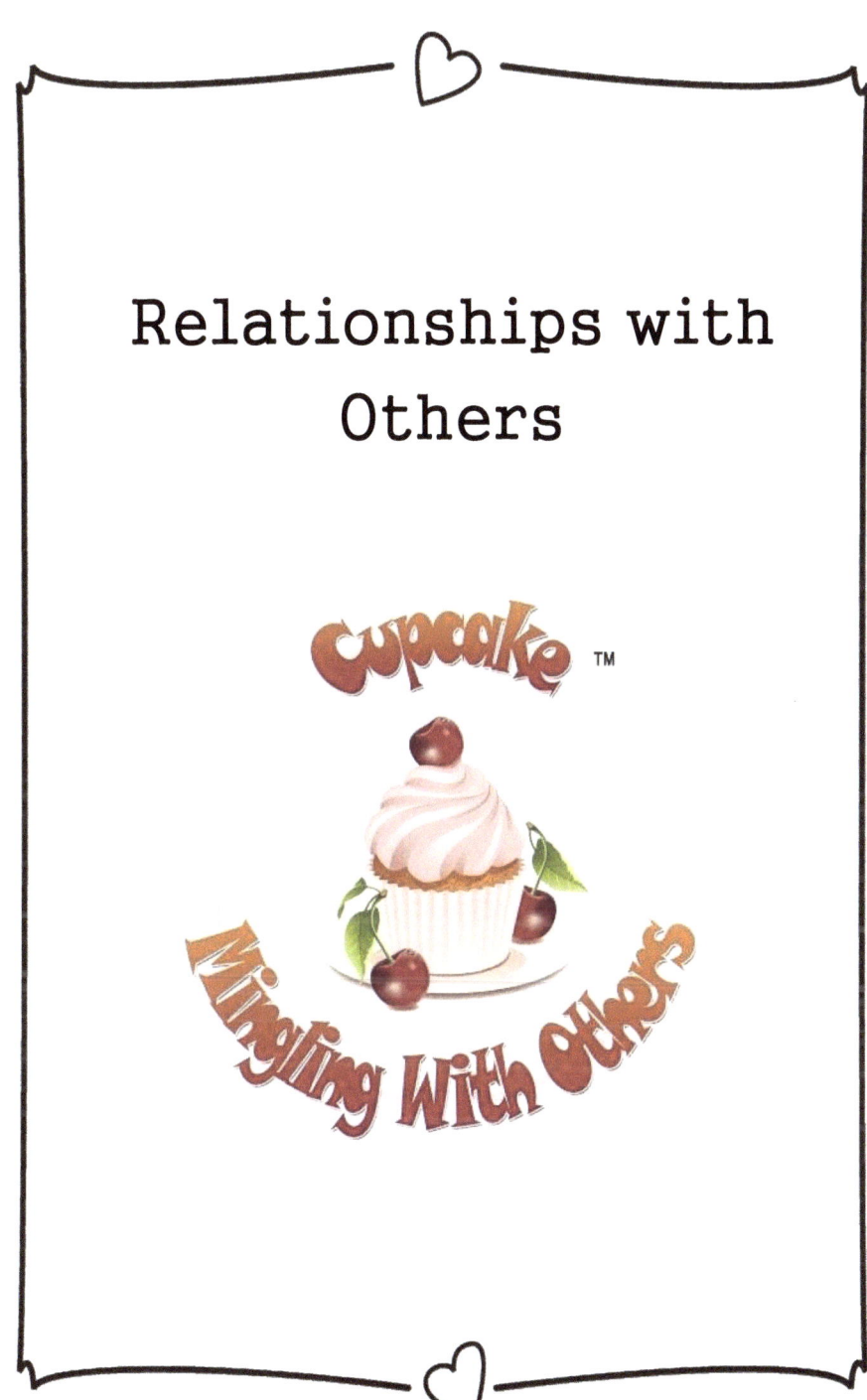

CUP CAKE - RELATIONSHIPS WITH OTHERS

ARE YOU READY FOR A RELATIONSHIP?

Now that you have spent time getting to know "YOURSELF', and you have a "new perspective" on who you are and what you need to be happy, you now have the proper tools to start mingling and socializing with others with the understanding that the overall goal of keeping the people who are for you, and those who are not and you should keep them at a distance on the other side of the boundary you will need to establish.

When meeting other people, you now have to start applying the tools you learned about yourself during the Cake Pop section, on others. That means, you have to recreate some new habits and behaviors when it comes to communicating because your old habits were not as effective. Relationships are like baking a great cake. You can't bake a cake with the wrong ingredients and you can't establish a long lasting, healthy, loving relationship with sabotaging communication skills. In order to achieve that goal, women have to start communicating their needs instead of just believing things will get better with time because they will eventually figure you out. If you don't learn how to read people, you will find yourself frustrated all the time. Because no two people think the same way about everything, until you take the time needed to get to know them, you will find yourself in frustrating situations trying to get them to think like you when they might not be able to. When it comes to relationships, women need to know how to read men, like they read women! Men analyze and study women so they can determine the best approach to get to know them. Men listen intently to the information you are sharing with them so they can figure out what makes you tick. Unfortunately, many men do this NOT to learn what it will take to make you happy, but to learn your weaknesses so they can take advantage of you, use you, and get you to take care of them. It's easy to get a man. The real work is getting and keeping the right one! The 80/20 Reflection-Meter is a concept I created to help people determine if they are ready to be in a healthy relationship. The things outlined in this section are all of the communication barriers and challenges you need to overcome if you desire to be in a long lasting relationship. Now that you have figured out what you need to be happy (which includes not exhibiting unhealthy communication methods), the key to understanding others is

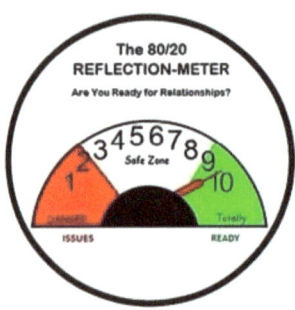

1) Determine what they need to be happy, then

2) Determine if you can fulfill their needs,

3) Without losing yourself in the process and the very first thing to know about a relationship is understanding what a relationship is.

IF I CAN'T BE THE CAKE, I WON'T BE THE CRUMZ

CUP CAKE - RELATIONSHIPS WITH OTHERS

1. WHAT IS "REVELATION" IN A RELATIONSHIP?

The book, *"The Complete Husband"* states in order to begin a relationship with someone, you must first understand exactly what a relationship is. *A relationship is a covenant of companionship with someone else. A companion is that person with whom one enters into close union with. Someone with whom you are INTIMATELY united in thoughts, goals, plans, efforts, and in the case of marriage, your body.* One major pre-requisite to a relationship is REVELATION. In order for us to know God, he had to REVEAL Himself to us through the inspired writings by the authors of the books in the Bible. If it was not for the Bible, we would not know how to establish a personal relationship with God through his son Jesus Christ. However, when it comes to our relationships with others, we may find it difficult to reveal ourselves because of the personal hindrances we face such as;

1) Fear - being afraid to reveal your "true" self to others because they may reject you. When you don't learn how to be honest and truthful as a child, you grow up accepting lies as the truth because of the rejection you may receive if you don't go along with them.

2) Selfishness - When you are not comfortable sharing your truth with others, you are in turn acting selfishly because the fear you are experiencing is causing you to withdraw from the person or the people you care about.

3) Pride - When you keep people from being honest with you, you are actually keeping them from telling you how they feel. Even if their feelings might not be accurate, it is still the best practice to let them share what is on their heart. When you keep people from offering their true disclosure, you are choosing to accept only your views about those things which in essence cause you to be prideful. When you walk around with blinders on, you force people to lie to you.

4) Laziness and **5) Ignorance** are probably the two issues that keep people from revealing themselves to others because of the IGNORANCE of not knowing how much work is really involved in maintaining and sustaining a long lasting, loving, and healthy, relationship with someone else. When your mate is ignorant, they can't change their behavior because they don't know how. However; when they know different and refuse to change, their LAZINESS makes it appear they are unwilling to meet you half way. When your mate does not see how important these things are to you, their "ignorance" and "laziness" make them feel unavailable to you. Once you learn how to identify and navigate these barriers that keep you both from revealing yourself to one another, you can establish healthy communication techniques with your mate.

The Complete Husband: Louis Paul Priolo, Calvary Press (August 22, 2007)

IF I CAN'T BE THE CAKE, I WON'T BE THE CRUMZ

2. MY GRANDMOTHER'S THREE MONTH RELATIONSHIP RULE

1ST MONTH IS SUGAR

When you first start dating someone, in the sugar phase, or the first month of your relationship, you both are nice, thoughtful, sweet, and loving. You both can't get enough of each other. Beware, of the honeymoon" phase because during this phase you both are always sweet as sugar. You haven't invested enough time into the relationship to see the "real" or "true" person. Time will reveal itself, but if you don't wait and give the relationship some time for them to truly "reveal" themselves, you will find yourself rushing into a bad situation that will be difficult to get out of.

2ND MONTH IS PIE

Now during the PIE phase or the 2nd month, you both start noticing thing's don't feel quite like they used too, but it is "too early' into the relationship for you to consider the issue a "big deal". During this period of your relationship, both parties are holding back how they really feel because they don't want to "scare" the person off. This is the best time to start sharing your concerns. Since there is no perfect person, if his heart is in the right place, when you both share your concerns, if they truly understand where you are coming from, they will respect your concerns and try to make appropriate adjustments. If they don't, and they continue the behaviors you have spoke with them about, that's the time to listen to the wisdom of

1st time shame of you. 2nd time shame on me.

Fool me once, shame on you, Fool me twice, shame on me.

Confrontation does not occur when two people agree. It occurs when they disagree. The best time to discuss your concerns is early in the relationship because you have not invested a great deal of time into it. If he's for you, he will work with you. If he's not, then on to PHASE THREE

3RD MONTH SO LONG, SEE YAH, GOODBYE
IF I CAN'T BE THE CAKE I WON'T BE THE CRUMZ
IF I CAN'T BE IT ALL
I'D RATHER HAVE NONE!

One day, two days, three days; One month, two months, three months; One year, two years, three years, regardless of the period of time, the PHASES are still the same. Learning how to work through Phase 2 to prevent Phase 3 is the key.

3. ARE THEY WORTHY OF YOUR HEART?

Now you can see why it is best to discuss your concerns early on. If you wait too long, you start to feel "invested" and begin to feel like you don't want to lose the valuable time you've invested into the relationship. A man who not only "hears" your concerns, but who is willing to work towards a resolution, is a man after your heart. A person who is selfish, self-centered, egotistical and only concerned about themselves will say you are being inconsiderate and selfish because you won't let them have their way. This same person does not see they are trying to get their way. Many times people want you to lose in the situation and they are not willing to lose as well. If two people can't see eye-to-eye, then they BOTH HAVE TO LOSE something. That's called compromise and meeting a person half way. We have to stop giving in and going along to get along. In the end, you find yourself unhappy, miserable, and depressed. You will never find happiness just because someone else is happy. The relationship should be reciprocal.

Dating is a way to **RELATE** or get to know a person.
To A MAN, **IT IS NOT AN INTERVIEW FOR A WIFE**. If HE did not ask you to be in a COMMITTED RELATIONSHIP with him YOU'RE NOT. Stop thinking dating is a pre-marriage interview. It is a way for him to see how well he relates or can communicate with you. One grave mistake many women today make is trying to raise, take care of, or help him to become a "Godly" man. Because it is a woman's nature to want to help her mate, when helping turns into taking over, you lose your sense of happiness trying to find happiness through them. According to Abram Maslow, if the first two basic needs like food, clothing, shelter, and safety are not met, it will be difficult for anyone to love you because these life essential needs are missing. You cannot give a man something he has not established for himself. Don't lose yourself trying to love someone who is NOT READY to love you back!

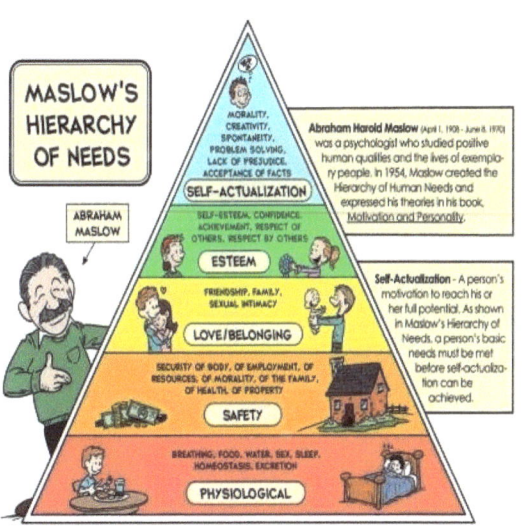

IF I CAN'T BE THE CAKE, I WON'T BE THE CRUMZ

4. IDENTIFYING A MAN WORTHY OF YOUR HEART

A man has faith and believes in a greater good.

A man respects himself and others.

A man is capable of providing for himself and his family.

A man is different from a boy because a man does what's RIGHT while a boy does WHAT FEELS GOOD.

A man basis his decisions on what's morally right versus what feels right and when struggling, will ask someone smarter and wiser for advice.

A man believes in himself, understands his weaknesses and strengths, but is not arrogant.

A man can admit when he is wrong, take ownership of the problem, and learn from his mistakes.

A man can be angry without being cruel or violent.

A man is not a coward and can defend himself if needed, but knows when to fight and when to walk away.

A man knows to treat a woman like a lady and give appropriate respect.

A man is able to truly love and be committed to that love.

A man does not betray his fellow man for personal gains.

A man is not afraid to be compassionate and affectionate.

A man can be sexual without being degrading or condescending.

A man understands self-sacrifice, doing good for another person even when there is no real benefit to one's self, to achieve a greater good. (i.e. Volunteer Fireman, EMT).

4. IDENTIFYING A MAN WORTHY OF YOUR HEART
continued

MANHOOD

As defined by a man: *"Manhood is the stage in life that a boy reaches after he matures from a boy to a man. It is defined by a man's ability to be responsible for and cover all he was given by the Lord to be responsible for. Specifically to lead, provide for, and to protect"*

FATHERHOOD

As defined by a man: *"Fatherhood is the natural order that takes place when a man with a son, daughter or a child placed in his care passes on, and teaches all he knows to his child or the children placed in his care all that God and those who raised him taught him. It is the passing on of the legacy of adulthood, and the equipping of young people to prepare them for life and the teaching of their own children to pass the same onto the generations to come."*

Ladies, know the difference!

R = RESPECTFUL to others
E = Not afraid to show his EMOTIONS
A = Equally AFFECTIONATE & APPRECIATIVE to his family
L = LISTENS with intent, especially to his wife and kids
M = Well MANNERED and polite
E = EARNING his own way through life
N = NEAT and clean (not a slob or a pig)

He who finds a wife finds what is good and receives favor from the LORD (Proverbs 18:22)." The hardest thing for women to do is to wait for him to find you. But in essence, that is the only way you'll know for sure that his heart is into the relationship. **LET HIM FIND YOU** for the reasons identified in this section. If he "chooses" you, then he will appreciate the relationship because the true nature of a man is to be the "head" of the family and to feel that he is capable to lead and provide for them. If you "choose" or "pursue" him, then you are already out of order in the relationship because as a man, he already does not feel as though you can trust him to make his own decisions.

IF I CAN'T BE THE CAKE, I WON'T BE THE CRUMZ

5. IDENTIFYING A GODLY MAN

EPHESIANS 5:22-33

25 Husbands, love your wives, <u>just as Christ loved the church and gave himself up for her</u>
26 to make <u>her holy,</u> cleansing [a] <u>her by the washing</u> with water through the word,
27 and to present <u>her to himself</u> as a radiant church, without stain or wrinkle or any other blemish, but holy and blameless.
28 **In this same way, husbands ought to love their wives as their own bodies. He who loves his wife loves himself**.
29 **After all, no one ever hated their own body, but they feed and care for their body, just as Christ does the church**
30 for we are members of his body.
31 "For this reason a man will leave his father and mother and be united to his wife, and the two will become one flesh."[b]
32 This is a profound mystery—but I am talking about Christ and the church.
33 However, **each one of you also must love his wife as he loves himself , and the wife must respect her husband**.

MY ANALOGY OF THESE VERSUS

The CHURCH IS THE BRIDE OF CHRIST
Husbands are to LOVE their wives as Christ loved the Church or HIS BRIDE
Husbands are to respect the Church
Husbands are to Love the Church
Husbands are to Revere the Church
Husbands are to "CHERISH" the Church
Husbands are to CLEAVE to their wives
Husbands are to Forsake all others for their wives
Husbands are to be the HEAD in their homes

SO CAKE POPS & CUP CAKES By HUMAN NATURE most men can't give you this until you are in fact HIS WIFE.

Also note, a marriage that is ordained by God will last the test and trials of time. A marriage that is due to your fleshly desires will not. We must start heeding to God's will and not our flesh's. If his character does not line up with the will of God for a husband, then you will experience heartache and pain in the relationship. Just because he goes to church does not necessarily make him marriage material. However, you can learn how to compliment and support him which in turn can encourage him to become the man God wants him to be. However, he has to want it. You can support it, but God and him are the only ones who can make it happen.

6. MEN ARE DEFINITELY FROM MARS

Now that he's found you, please understand that men are DEFINITELY by nature different than women. If you ask ten men their views on one subject, they would generally give you the same answer. If you ask ten women the same question, you'd get twenty-five different answers. Men regardless of their age, generally think alike about most subjects. Women have to stop trying to change men and first work on UNDERSTANDING them. The biggest frustration you will hear from married women is how they want their husbands to "communicate" and "talk to them more." Women want their men to share how they feel about "everything" like their intimate thoughts, their frustrations, what affects them, and especially what would make them happy. The request that comes naturally to women seems to be the hardest thing for men to give. Ladies, the issue is not that the men in your life can't give you the desires of our heart; we just have to talk to them in a language they understand. In the book *"Men are from Mars, Women are from Venus"* written in 1974, Dr. John Gray's perspective about the human nature of women versus men helped me understand when it came to men, I had to communicate differently in order to communicate effectively with them. The following chapters helped me the most:

About Men
About Women
Mr. Fix It
Men go to their caves, women need to talk
Men are like rubber bands
Discovering our emotional needs
How to avoid arguments
Scoring points with the opposite sex

101 ways for men to score points with a woman
Define your list!
How to ask for support and get it

What I learned the most about women versus men, is that most men think in black and white, while women think in shades of gray. The reason men will have the same solution for one question is because they are wired differently than us. Their answers are typically black and white. The reason women will have more answers than men about the same question is because we tend to "over analyze" a problem. Just like there are many shades of gray, women have that many views and opinions about a topic. Purchase the book so you can understand the secret to get men to respond and give you what you desire, while at the same time, learn how to get him to listen and HEAR you when you talk!

Men are from Mars, Women are from Venus, Dr. John Gray, Prentice Hall Press; 1St Edition (January 17, 2007)

7. GETTING HIM TO LISTEN WHEN YOU TALK

The true nature of a man is for his woman to be happy. A woman should not only desire to be loved by her husband, she should want to be "cherished" by him as the scripture outlines. Men, desire to be the provider and protector over their loved ones, but today, the rules that works in one home, may be different than someone else's. Today, couples need to work together to define the rules that will work in their relationship. Some women are better at managing the finances than their mate. Some couples choose to define which bills will be paid by whom and they manage their financial responsibilities that way. What works for some couples may not necessarily work for others, but the goal should be for the two of you to work "together" at finding a process that works for your relationship. I remind my husband of the saying "Happy Wife, Happy Life" all the time. But I am also mindful of my role as his help mate who is constantly reminding myself to be mindful of his needs as well. Relationships should never be one sided, but in order for a man to "cherish" his wife, he must feel safe, secure, and be respected in his relationship by her. If a wife tears down her house with her hands or the words from her mouth, then her husband won't find his home a place of refuge; but a place under siege. When a woman ensures her husband is respected, appreciated, and cared for emotionally, psychologically, and yes physically, then it helps him to ensure her needs are being met. When it comes to marriage, the only difference between being married (Mrs. Cake), or being single (Ms. Cake Pop) or dating (Ms. Cup Cake) is that the married woman understands the true meaning of SUBMISSION!

8. SUBMISSION

Submission is the process of

1) Recognizing something that has been said or done has upset or hurt you
2) Choosing not to act out in rage
3) Seeking God's grace and wisdom when you are upset
4) So that the Holy Spirit can speak to you and you will hear, and head to what He is asking of you in that moment.
5) Many times, the Holy Spirit will tell you to "walk away". Will you trust the Holy Spirit, or respond in your flesh?

Submission is not giving in or giving up. It is learning how to pick your battles and determine the right time to have a crucial conversation. When someone hurts you, or makes you upset or angry, your response to their behavior may come as a surprise to them because they did not see it as something offensive. If you respond in an attacking manner, you will not get to the root of the problem which is to speak to your reason for feeling upset. If you can't tell them why it upsets you in a calm manner, you can't identify solutions to fix the problem. Your walking away is not forever. It's just for that moment or until you can calm down and get a grasp on your pain. Then you can schedule a day and time to discuss the issue rationally with them. When you calm down, you can identify the reason for your pain, identify solutions to resolve the problem, and speak with them at an appropriate date/time. People need you to help them understand why you are upset and how to fix the problem. Your reflecting on the problem, and solution gives them something to work with. When you see them trying to fix the behavior, then you know they are willing to meet you half way. If they don't show an effort to change, then you can recognize the need for boundaries with them.

Submission and seeking God's revelation about how to handle the problem is the only way to identify a solution that works favorably for both parties. But if you don't seek God first, you will respond in your flesh and the consequences of that response can be harder to fix than your simply choosing to walk away. Wait on the Lord, because the Holy Spirit will be there with you if you let Him.

REFLECTION SCRIPTURES

BOOK	SCRIPTURE
Matthew 5:11-12	When people misread your intentions
Luke 12:13-21	When you are tempted to look out only for #1
Matthew 16:25	When selfishness gets you in its grip
1 Peter 1:6-7	When you suffer for doing right
Matthew 6:14-15	When someone has harmed you
Matthew 7	When you are tempted to look down on others

CUP CAKE - RELATIONSHIPS WITH OTHERS

REFLECTIONS FROM CLIENTS

Pay more attention during conversations and not jumping before the broom

♡

I'm going to be more patient throughout our relationship

♡

Being able to learn and accept constructive relationship concepts

♡

Learn to listen instead of taking charge

♡

I am able to accept my faults

♡

To change the way I approach others

♡

I will remember and not expect a man to think like a woman

♡

Cake Chronicles shows the erroneous assumptions women make in dealing with men

♡

Realize I'm the opposite of a man

♡

Reality of Man vs. Woman

♡

Change the way of communicating when it comes to men

CUP CAKE - RELATIONSHIPS WITH OTHERS

THINGS TO KEEP DOING

_____
_____
_____
_____
_____
_____
_____

THINGS TO START DOING

_____
_____
_____
_____
_____
_____
_____

THINGS TO STOP DOING

_____
_____
_____
_____
_____
_____
_____

IF I CAN'T BE THE CAKE, I WON'T BE THE CRUMZ

CUP CAKE - RELATIONSHIPS WITH OTHERS

MY 80/20 CUPCAKE CHECKLIST

- ☐ I will try to have patience with others even when we disagree
- ☐ I recognize relationships take work by both parties, not just me
- ☐ I will be mindful of the words and actions I use to provoke others
- ☐ I will not settle for less than my 80%
- ☐ I will put my safety and my children's safety first (Always)

OTHER NOTES

_____
_____
_____
_____
_____
_____
_____
_____
_____
_____
_____
_____
_____
_____
_____
_____
_____

IF I CAN'T BE THE CAKE, I WON'T BE THE CRUMZ

CUP CAKE - RELATIONSHIPS WITH OTHERS

HELLO FRIEND

*I really wasn't looking for you,
now you say I'm taking you through changes
is that what you think I do?
When I just met you and
rearrange my time to spend with you.*

*I'm taking you through changes, who me?
When you said, "You had everything you need"
Now I feel like a court case
with my feelings that I plead.*

*Don't Let this change you speak of twist the facts,
and let the verdict be in
I need to be me,
not trying to change anything
we can just be friends.*

*We can embrace what we have
and like what we do
sharing real feelings in that space
At the end of the day,
when my yay is yay and your nay is nay
keep it real in that place.*

*So without a doubt we will know that you was you,
and I was me and we laugh to the break of dawn
But changes, oh no I won't co-sign to that
I just met you, not trying to change you
Like children in the sandbox
I'm just trying have some fun finding a new friend.*

By Riah (2017)

IF I CAN'T BE THE CAKE, I WON'T BE THE CRUMZ

MRS CAKE
I'M MARRIED

IF I CAN'T BE THE CAKE, I WON'T BE THE CRUMZ

WHAT IS MARRIAGE?

A marriage is at its best when both partners view each other as equals in respect and importance. When both the man and the woman come together to lean upon one another in equality, a relationship is given the opportunity to flourish and grow in the most ideal situations. The two must work every day to understand their partner's needs and even their wants. The relationship cannot thrive if it is one-sided because someone will feel robbed or unloved if their needs are not being met. That is why it is important for couples to know what their 80/20 is as an individual, then understand what their partner's 80/20 is, and work daily to fulfill the minimum emotional, psychological, and physical needs in their relationship.

At the heart of a marriage is COMMUNICATION and identifying what your mate needs to be happy. The hardest thing to do when communicating with others is learning how to hear them instead of listening to them. There are seven scriptures in the Bible where God wants us to understand the importance of HEARING and not just listening. The phrase hear appears seven times in the gospels; eight if you count Mark 4:23. Two are duplicates of Matthew 13:9 having to do with the Sower and the seed. A variation, "he who has an ear" appears seven times in Revelations 2-3, and another version, "let the reader understand" appears in Matthew 24:15. These words, only used by the Lord, seem to underscore something important. It's as if God is saying, ***"Pay attention now. This part is NOT optional and is IMPORTANT"*** Adding them up gives us 14 passages that are required of the believer to hear and not just listen. When God says the phrase "He who has an ear, let them hear", He wants us to understand the difference between listening and hearing. When you hear, you receive the information not only in your ear gate, but in your heart, and you work to "transform" or change your behavior. When it comes to communicating with others, it is important that both parties understand how to:

1) Communicate your needs,

2) Balance giving your partner what they "NEED" instead of you THINK they need",

3) and know how not to lose yourself in the process!!

THAT'S THE KEY

DEALING WITH BLENDED FAMILIES

Another aspect of relationships and marriages that should be addressed is the "blended family" dynamic. When two individuals come together and establish a family with children from another relationship, the hardest thing to manage is how the "new" parent will engage the children, and establish healthy, respectful and loving boundaries with them. One approach I found helpful in my blended family was to first pray with my husband about the issue within the family that concerned me. I first discussed the issue with my husband so that we could identify a solution for the problem together. Once we identified a solution together, we then called a family meeting with everyone where we started the meeting off with a prayer asking the Lord to allow us to have an ear to hear and understand what is being said, and for us to collectively and lovingly respect one another. Then we discussed the issue with everyone present and worked to have an understanding about how the "family" will try to fix the problem.

Prayer helps to set the atmosphere and encourages everyone to feel safe to offer their views and opinions so they can feel included in the process. I highly recommend having family meetings at least once a month to discuss positive things that are going on in the family, as well as to provide an opportunity for the family to discuss their concerns in an environment where the kids and young adults feel safe to share their "truth." However, keep in mind that the parents might need to define the best approach for the issue even when the children/or young adults have given their views and opinions. Offering them a platform to discuss their concerns does not always mean they will be happy with the outcome. This process teaches them the value of being heard, as well as how to cope with rejection in a healthy manner especially when rejection is a fact of life.

If you build a relationship where there are young adults and/or teenagers, it can take some time before you all establish a healthy respect for one another. When I married my husband, I recognized his teenage children still needed their mother's support so for every important holiday and life event, she was invited. Her and I discussed what was going on with the kids because she had an important role to play in their lives like I did. I also recognize if she wasn't involved, then they could manipulate the three of us and I knew that was not in our best interest. Once the kids became young adults with their lives and living in their own homes, there was no longer a need for us to communicate about the kids. We are still very cordial and she still gets invited to "some" family functions. I realize for some women and their unique situation, it may not be possible to be this cordial with your husband's ex, but for the sake of the kids and the family, it is what is wise.

DEALING WITH EXTENDED FAMILY MEMBERS

Juggling the concerns and issues identified by extended family members can be an influential challenge unless both partners are prepared and have agreed on the approach for how much involvement the family has into their relationship and personal affairs. You both have to talk and be realistic about family members that can potentially cause a divide in your relationship. Extended family members will feel they have a right to show love and concern for their loved one, however, they have to be told the importance for them to respect your choices and decisions about the matter. When you love someone, you care about their well-being, but you also have to respect their choices. In-laws (especially mother-in-laws and father-in-laws) can try to influence your relationship but they will only succeed if their child does not establish healthy boundaries with them. *"Therefore a man shall leave his father and mother and be joined (cleave) to his wife, and they shall become one flesh" (Genesis 2:24).* You can love your parents, respect them, and establish healthy boundaries all at the same time. The hardest and necessary process is to lovingly ask them to respect your decisions and to pray for you when they don't agree with them. Many times they have to learn how to let go and let God!

THE PROVERS 31

The Biblical account of the ideal "Godly" woman can be found in the book of Proverbs with the Proverbs 31 Virtuous Woman. Many Christian women ask themselves if it is truly possible for a woman to be the Proverbs 31 Virtuous woman. Let's take a look at the scripture in its entirety, and then reflect on the scriptures in a way that helps us to identify and relate with others as a virtuous woman. When I read the scriptures, outlined in Proverbs 31:10 - 31, a theme stood out to me about her relationship to HERSELF, to HER HUSBAND, to HER FAMILY, and then to OTHERS. Review the scriptures below, and then ask yourself what stands out to you about this woman of NOBLE character. Then review the scriptures based on each theme, and think about the things you can KEEP and to START doing so you can begin living the life of a woman of noble character, and what do you need to STOP DOING that is not in alignment as a woman of God. After reading each section, review the reflection from my clients, and then note your own personal reflections on the pages provided.

THE PROVERS 31 WOMAN - TO HERSELF

10 [a]A wife of noble character who can find? She is worth far more than rubies.
13 She selects wool and flax and works with eager hands.
14 She is like the merchant ships, bringing her food from afar.
16 She considers a field and buys it; out of her earnings she plants a vineyard.
17 She sets about her work vigorously; her arms are strong for her tasks.
18 She sees that her trading is profitable, and her lamp does not go out at night.
19 In her hand she holds the distaff and grasps the spindle with her fingers.
22 She makes coverings for her bed; she is clothed in fine linen and purple.
24 She makes linen garments and sells them, and supplies the merchants with sashes.
25 She is clothed with strength and dignity; she can laugh at the days to come.
26 She speaks with wisdom, and faithful instruction is on her tongue.
29 "Many women do noble things, but you surpass them all."
30 Charm is deceptive, and beauty is fleeting; but a woman who fears the Lord is to be praised.
31 Honor her for all that her hands have done, and let her works bring her praise at the city gate.

THE PROVERS 31 WOMAN - TO HERSELF
CLIENT REFLECTIONS

THINGS TO KEEP DOING

⇒ *Communication*
⇒ *Hard working and independence*
⇒ *Speaking with wisdom and faithful instruction on your tongue*
⇒ *Seeking God Direction and putting him first and getting closer to Him*
⇒ *Pursuing my dreams and goals*
⇒ *Self respect & High Self Esteem*
⇒ *Loving the Lord*
⇒ *The Peace and my faith*
⇒ *Being me and minding my business*
⇒ *Honesty in love*
⇒ *Always being truthful*
⇒ *Doing what makes you happy if it has been working for you*

THINGS TO START DOING

⇒ *Giving more of me to MYSELF (ME TIME)*
⇒ *Listening and thinking before I speak*
⇒ *Encouraging younger women*
⇒ *Loving others*
⇒ *Setting goals for myself*
⇒ *Making changes to improve my situation*
⇒ *Being more sincere about my walk with God*

THINGS TO STOP DOING

⇒ *Reacting so quickly*
⇒ *Telling myself what I can't do*
⇒ *Feeling like I'm not enough*
⇒ *Being foolish about anything*
⇒ *Being so hard on myself and shutting down*

THE PROVERS 31 WOMAN - HERSELF
YOUR REFLECTIONS

_____
_____
_____
_____
_____
_____
_____

THINGS TO START DOING

_____
_____
_____
_____
_____
_____
_____

THINGS TO STOP DOING

_____
_____
_____
_____
_____
_____
_____

THE PROVERS 31 WOMAN - WITH HER HUSBAND
CLIENT REFLECTIONS

11 Her husband has full confidence in her and lacks nothing of value.

12 She brings him good, not harm, all the days of her life.

23 Her husband is respected at the city gate, where he takes his seat among the elders of the land.
28 Her husband calls her blessed also, and he praises her:

KEEP & START DOING

⇒ *Bringing him good, not harm, all the days of our lives*
⇒ *Validating him more*
⇒ *Speaking directly to him when I am hurt, rather than letting it fester.*
⇒ *Talking about my thoughts, fears, feelings and ideas*
⇒ *Getting to know each other better*
⇒ *Understanding his Love Language*
⇒ *Trying to build trust*
⇒ *Complimenting him and being honest with him*
⇒ *Being an encourager and tell him how much he is appreciated*
⇒ *Keep respecting his boundaries*

THINGS TO STOP DOING

⇒ *Complaining and trying to chastise my husband. He is not my son!*
⇒ *Putting him off and tuning out*
⇒ *Being the one to give in*
⇒ *Punishing my husband for the things he does not know about or any wrong doing*
⇒ *Putting outsiders in*
⇒ *Speaking when he is talking*
⇒ *Expecting him to be my everything*
⇒ *Thinking that the next man is like the last one*
⇒ *Criticizing even if it is done nicely*

THE PROVERS 31 WOMAN - WITH HER HUSBAND
YOUR REFLECTIONS

THINGS TO KEEP DOING

_____
_____
_____
_____
_____
_____

THINGS TO START DOING

_____
_____
_____
_____
_____
_____

THINGS TO STOP DOING

_____
_____
_____
_____
_____
_____
_____
_____

THE PROVERS 31 WOMAN - HER FAMILY
CLIENT REFLECTIONS

15 She gets up while it is still night;

21 When it snows, she has no fear for her household; for all of them are clothed in scarlet.

27 She watches over the affairs of her household and does not eat the bread of idleness.

28 Her children arise and call her blessed; her husband also, and he praises her:

28 Her children arise and call her blessed

THINGS TO KEEP & START DOING

- *Having better relationships with the women in my family*
- *Praying for my lost son*
- *Sharing the Goodness of the Lord through testimonies and confessions*
- *Being in the background more so that my kids can be an adult. But be there when needed*
- *Telling them I love them*
- *Allowing them to make their own mistakes*
- *Stop putting the children father down in front of them*
- *Showing consideration to my grandchildren*
- *Praying with our children*
- *Spending more time with extended family*

THINGS TO STOP DOING

- *Spending so much time away from home*
- *Getting into conversations that does not include me*
- *Trying to force Christ on them*
- *Trying to be everything to them. Trying to catch their slack*
- *Trying to live my grown children's lives*
- *Letting a negative situation helping others deter me*
- *Family from finding fault with my praise*
- *Putting them before myself*
- *Taking sides with family and being the peace maker*
- *Being so judgmental*

THE PROVERS 31 WOMAN - HER FAMILY
YOUR REFLECTIONS

THINGS TO KEEP DOING

_____
_____
_____
_____
_____
_____

THINGS TO START DOING

_____
_____
_____
_____
_____
_____
_____
_____

THINGS TO STOP DOING

_____
_____
_____
_____
_____
_____
_____
_____

THE PROVERS 31 WOMAN - TO OTHERS
CLIENT REFLECTIONS

*15 she provides food for her family
and portions for her female servants.*

20 She opens her arms to the poor and extends her hands to the needy.

THINGS TO KEEP & START DOING

- *Working hard to provide for my son*
- *Ministering to other women*
- *Making my home a safe haven of love, peace, and tranquility*
- *Helping others*
- *Networking and being around people that are positive and have Jesus in their lives*
- *Learning how to deal with different situations*
- *Loving others*
- *Praying for those I have an issue with*

THINGS TO STOP DOING

- *Always being there for others*
- *Looking for a man*
- *Saying hurtful things just to win an argument*
- *Gossip, hating others and jealousy*
- *Looking at man*
- *Arguing*
- *Being content with just 20. Trying to make 20 into 80*
- *Stop believing false words (lies)*
- *Listening to dream killers*
- *Complaining and tuning out*
- *Being so willing to give up my place*
- *Thinking a man can complete me*
- *I should have stopped the relationship before it got started*

THE PROVERS 31 WOMAN - TO OTHERS
YOUR REFLECTION

THINGS TO KEEP DOING

_____
_____
_____
_____
_____

THINGS TO START DOING

_____
_____
_____
_____
_____
_____
_____
_____

THINGS TO STOP DOING

_____
_____
_____
_____
_____
_____
_____
_____

VIRTUOUS WOMAN CHECKLIST

Becoming the Proverbs 31 Woman takes time. It is not something to be mastered, but with practice it becomes a part of your character and nature. Do what is required of you for God, then yourself, then your children, then our family, then others. Let God take care of what is required of your mate or your husband.

I am His Suitable Helper
I am a Virtuous Wife; a Wife of Valor
I am a Devoted Wife
I am the Builder of My House
I am Full of Purpose as I Build
I Find Great Satisfaction in Building My Home
I am his Encourager
I Honor and Respect My Husband
I am Adaptable
I Follow My Husband's Guidance
I am One with My Husband
My Love Story is a Reflection of Jesus Love for Us All
I Follow Christ's Example in the Way that I Love
My Marriage is Holy
I am a Covenant Keeper
I keep my Heart Clear
I Handle Conflict Correctly
I am My Husband's Crown
I am My Husband's Glory
I am a Trophy Wife
I am Strong and Graceful
I am a Woman who Fears the Lord
I am Blessed
I am a Fruitful Vine Within My House
I am a Watchman
My Oil Keeps Burning
My Lamp Stays Lit
I Excel
I am Submitting to the Process
I Face the Future with a Smile

Donna Partow, Becoming the Woman God Wants Me to Be: A 90-Day Guide to Living the Proverbs 31 Life by Donna Partow (1-Jun-2008), Revell (1 Jun. 2008) (1600)

REFLECTION SCRIPTURES

BOOK	SCRIPTURE
Ephesians 5:22-24	When there are troubles with your husband
Ephesians 5:25-30	When you are troubling your husband
1 Philippians 4:4-8	Living virtuously
1 Corinthians 9:25	Be prepared as your life is no your own
Hebrews 13:4	Marriage bed should be kept pure
Mark 10:6-9	What god has joined together, no man can separate
Proverbs 5:15-19	May you always be a blessing to your husband
1 Corinthians 13:4-8	The definition of Love
Ephesians 5:33	Husbands loving their wives as themselves
Genesis 2:24	Husbands and wives become one
Provebrs 19:14	A prudent wife is from the Lord

REFLECTIONS FROM CLIENTS

Learning that I am a "Cake" in his eyes

Being more honest with my feelings

How to communicate better with my husband

MY 80/20 MRS. CAKE CHECKLIST

- [ ] I will be transparent, honest, and truthful with my husband
- [ ] I will be honest with myself
- [ ] I will work daily on my relationship with my husband
- [ ] I will honor our vows and my charge as Godly woman/wife
- [ ] God, Myself, Family, Others. In that order always

OTHER NOTES

MRS. CAKE - I'M MARRIED

GOD GAVE ME MORE

I asked the Lord for someone
who would not break my heart
God gave me more

He gave me someone who cherishes my heart
and whose own heart is as pure as gold
I prayed for someone
who would be my soulmate
God gave me more

He gave me a confidante, a supporter and
a best friend
I waited for someone who would
truly appreciate me
God gave me more

He gave me someone full of compassion
and who's completely devoted to me
I trusted God to give me someone
who loves unconditionally
God blessed me with more

He blessed me with
a love of a lifetime
I hoped God would give me someone
with a sense of humor
God gave me more

He gave me someone
whose heartfelt laughter
brings me joy everyday
I believed God would
honor my sacrifices
God gave me more

He gave me someone who supports me
beyond my wildest dreams
God has surpassed my hopes,
eclipsed my dreams,
and exceeded all that I had envisioned
Just when I was about to give up
on finding true love
The Lord ushered you in

Little did I know
that the Lord
was preparing a feast for me
with everything I wanted
plus a whole lot more
I asked the Lord
For a companion
God gave me more

HE GAVE ME YOU

By L.R. Highsmith, Ascension into Love, Lucreations

IF I CAN'T BE THE CAKE, I WON'T BE THE CRUMZ

CRUMZY SITUATIONS
A RANGE OF UNHEALTHY EMOTIONS

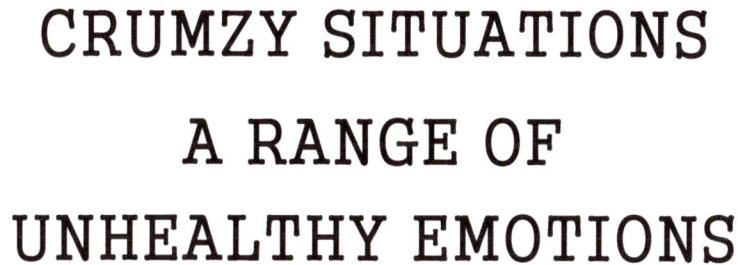

IF I CAN'T BE THE CAKE, I WON'T BE THE CRUMZ

WHAT ARE CRUMZY SITUATIONS?

Feeling "Crumzy" or experiencing a Crumzy situation is when you find yourself dealing with an emotionally hurtful/painful situation, and you don't know how you got there. For instance, he moved on without you, and you don't know why or what happened. You find yourself wondering what went wrong or what you did to cause him to leave you. How about you need to move on but you haven't figured out why you are choosing to stay in the one-sided relationship. Many women find it hard to move on from a relationship where they are not happy and they know they are not getting their needs met because they are still holding on to the memory of the person he used to be. They try to snack on the leftovers or the Crumz because they remember how sweet the cake or the relationship used to be. But ladies, if you aren't the Cake, then being the Crumz won't cut it. Have you ever seen a cake recipe with ingredients flour, water and Crumz? No! Having self-esteem is not just about evaluating how you see yourself. It is also about understanding the behavior of those around you who are also struggling with liking themselves. People who have low self-esteem innately make you feel bad because they don't know how to handle their issues, so they project their drama and negative energy trying to influence you. If you are hanging out with a person that turns your positive energy and enthusiasm into negative emotions, you have to learn how to see it for what it really is. They are only deflecting guilt and blame on you which in turn, causes you to feel bad about yourself all for no reason!

The reason you define healthy boundaries with people is to guard and protect your heart and emotions. There's an old saying "Feed 'em from a long handled spoon." Start establishing boundaries so you can distance yourself from people who exhibit negative energy. Sometimes you have to start with the people closest to you, the people you call "family." Once you learn how to set boundaries with your immediate family, you will then feel empowered to set boundaries with others. Review the CRUMZY situations identified in this section to review some unhealthy types of relationships. The overall goal of this section is to encourage you to define your 80/20 and especially your 20. CRUMZY situations are instances when people do or say something you do not agree with and you feel offended by it. CRUMZY situations affect you as well as the others around you. Although you may be entitled to do what you want to do, your actions should not hurt others, especially those you love. And the actions of the people who say they love you shouldn't hurt you either!

ADULTS DEPENDING ON OTHER PEOPLE

MEN WHO DEPEND ON WOMEN

When teenagers are not given the proper tools to help them prepare for adulthood, they find themselves afraid to make minor or even major life decisions because they fear failing or being rejected so they choose an easier path by having their basic needs like food, shelter, and even their utilities provided by someone else. When a woman dates a man who is living with "family members," she should really ask herself why is he living with other people? Many men will say they are in transition from a previous relationship, yet they most likely have been living with someone else most of his life. There are many men who do not have their own home, or who are responsible for things such as rent/mortgage payments, and medical insurance. Men who find it difficult to provide for themselves were most likely coddled by their mothers, grandmother's, and other women in their lives. They need a woman who already is responsible for those basic needs so he does not have to financially contribute to them. When women establish boundaries and higher expectations of men, we will see a dramatic change in our men.

Now there are many exceptions to any rule, and thus there are some men who are truly in transition from an unhealthy relationship and need to establish themselves. It is okay to be in a relationship with someone who is going through this phase, but do not get caught up helping or rescuing him because of his situation. Don't be used, abused, and manipulated to provide and help him get where he "wants" to be. A real man will try to do that on his own. Someone who is not ready for the responsibilities of a relationship will try to mooch off of others and that is a person you should run from. WOMEN INCLUDED!

WOMEN WHO DEPEND ON OTHERS

There are some women who are afraid of being completely responsible for their basic needs just like the men identified above. ANYONE who does not have their basic needs established or the finances to maintain them on their own will use and manipulate people to get money from others so they can get whatever their desires met.

Please note, adults who depend on others display "jealousy" when others receive from the person why expect to take care of them. Even if the other people are their children. Be careful you're desire to help the children doesn't cause their parents to become envious of your actions. The children are the people who suffer the most when that happens.

FRIENDS VS. ACQUAINTANCES
KNOW THE DIFFERENCE

Social media is full of people that should be called "acquaintances" and not friends. People you know in passing, or someone you might like what they have shared online is not necessarily your friend. A friend is someone who respects and appreciates you for being the person you are. Even if the two of you do not see eye-to-eye on all subject matters, you both can agree to disagree or set healthy, respectable boundaries with one another. Proverbs 18:24 says, *"There is a friend who sticks closer than a brother."* The concept of friendship is outlined nine times in Proverbs. Wisdom is called a friend *(7:4), a friend loves at all times (17:17), a poor man is deserted by his friend (19:4), everyone is a friend to a man who gives gifts (19:6), a person with gracious speech has the king as his friend (22:11), faithful are the wounds of a friend (27:6), the sweetness of a friend comes from his earnest counsel (27:9), and do not forsake your friend and father's friend (27:10).* Based on these scriptures, there are two types of people "An acquaintance *who exists because you have something to offer them and a friend who genuinely loves and appreciates you.* Discern the difference between these two types of people and who you consider A FRIEND!

James 3:18-22: *"But no human being can tame the tongue. It is a restless evil, full of deadly poison. With it we bless our Lord and Father, and with it we curse people who are made in the likeness of God. From the same mouth come blessing and cursing. My brothers, these things ought not to be so. Does a spring pour forth from the same opening both fresh and salt water? Can a fig tree, my brothers, bear olives, or a grapevine produce figs? Neither can a salt pond yield fresh water. "*

Matthew 7:12: *"So whatever you wish that others would do to you, do also to them, for this is the Law and the Prophets."*

Leviticus 19:16-18: *"You shall not go around as a slanderer among your people, and you shall not stand up against the life of your neighbor: I am the Lord. "You shall not hate your brother in your heart, but you shall reason frankly with your neighbor, lest you incur sin because of him. You shall not take vengeance or bear a grudge against the sons of your own people, but you shall love your neighbor as yourself: I am the Lord. "*

Romans 13:10: *"Love does no wrong to a neighbor; therefore love is the fulfilling of the law. "*

Galatians 6:10: *"So then, as we have opportunity, let us do good to everyone, and especially to those who are of the household of faith. "*

STAYING FOR THE CHILDREN OR FOR MONEY

STAYING FOR THE CHILDREN

One of the hardest thing to do is admit YOU WERE WRONG! Many times women stay in unhealthy relationships because they have lost sight of their own goals, dreams, and desires. Someone or both parties are choosing to stay together because they believe it is in the "best interest" of the kids when what you are really doing is teaching the kids how to live and accept an unhealthy, unhappy relationship with others!

Children treat others how they have been treated or how they see their parents and adults in their lives treat others. The formative years for teenagers is the time when they are building friendships and relationships with others and their parents and family members are the first teachers of what is acceptable and even unacceptable behavior in those relationships. Teenagers rebel against their parents because they do not feel as if they have a voice or opinion about the issues that concern them in their home so they act out in order to get attention. If your relationship with your spouse is not working out, do not stay for the kids because they deserve to grow up in a home where everyone is loved, feels appreciated, and feel like a member of the household. It just may be in their best interest to receive that love from two households instead of one, especially if the adults in the house do not believe they can live in harmony and love with one another.

STAYING FOR THE MONEY

It is said that money is the root of all evil. When a person chases fame and fortune, they find themselves compromising their standards and their moral beliefs in order to do whatever is being asked of them just because they want the money. You should never want to forsake your safety and that of the people you love just because of your desire to have money, and you should never let money be the reason you choose to stay in an unhealthy relationship. God has equipped you with everything you need to take care of yourself, and therefore you should be prepared to take care of any financial matters on your own if the situation calls for it. People will manipulate you if they think you won't leave because of money or financial reasons. Never let money rule you.

SEPARATED OR MARRIED BUT LIVING LIKE YOU'RE SINGLE

Separation and divorce occur when the couple have not learned how to communicate their needs to one another. Someone or both parties are accepting things in the relationships that they really do not like which causes them to no longer want to be there. I do believe broken relationships can be restored if both parties do the following:

1.   IDENTIFY **YOUR PERSONAL** 80/20

Before the Cake Chronicles 80/20 Healthy Relationship Challenge, some people might not have ALL of the tools or ingredients that are needed to establish a healthy, loving, long-lasting relationship. Yes you need to have your checklist or your 80/20 prepared before you start dating or being in a relationship with others. You have to take the time to identify what you need to be happy, the things you don't like, and identify the unhealthy behaviors you bring to the relationship that are causing you to sabotage it. You won't know if the person you are interested in is capable of making you happy if you have not identified what happiness means to you! Once you have looked at yourself, then you have to proceed to the next step

2. LEARN **YOUR PARTNER'S** 80/20

Many married couples get together without understanding the significant importance of taking the time to learn their partner's 80/20. They have their own goals, dreams and desires and you have to respectfully get to know who he or she is as an individual.

If you believe you and your husband or mate are willing to do the work that is needed to repair your relationship, start over as a Cake Pop and complete the ingredients outlined in that section and have him do the same. Then evaluate and identify what your new CUP CAKE ingredients are GOING FORWARD in your newly defined relationship. You will both discover and uncover the missing ingredients that are needed in order to rebuild and redefine your marriage on terms where you both work to respect and appreciate one another. Marriage takes work ALL DAY EVERYDAY. For each new season of your life, you will constantly re-evaluate the new ingredients needed in order for your marriage to sustain the test of time. You both will have to be like the matrix and be "FLEXIBLE."

WHAT IS INTIMATE PARTNER VIOLENCE (IPV)

The term "intimate partner violence" includes the following acts as inflicted or caused by a current or former intimate partner:
⇒ Actual or threats of physical violence
⇒ Actual or threats of sexual violence
⇒ Emotional or psychological abuse (e.g., name-calling or putdowns, threats)
⇒ Stalking (e.g., excessive calls/texts/emails, monitoring daily activities, using technology to track a person's location)
⇒ Financial abuse (e.g., withholding money, ruining credit, stopping a partner from getting or keeping a job)
⇒ Threats to "out" a person's sexual orientation to family, work or friends

INTIMATE PARTNERS CAN INCLUDE
⇒ Current or former spouses
⇒ Boyfriends or girlfriends
⇒ Dating partners
⇒ Sexual partners
⇒ Domestic violence can occur in heterosexual and same-sex relationships.

STATISTICS
⇒ 85 percent of domestic abuse victims being women and 15 percent men.
⇒ 3 women murdered every day by a current or former male partner in the U.S.
⇒ 38,028,000 of women have experienced physical intimate partner violence in their lifetime.
⇒ Every minute 20 people are victims of intimate partner violence
⇒ 1 in 4 women will be victims of severe violence by an intimate partner in their lifetime.
⇒ 1 in 7 men will be victims of severe violence by an intimate partner in their lifetime.

No one should be subjected to violence from their partner. Seek assistance and learn your worth by setting boundaries and defining your 80/20.

DOMESTIC VIOLENCE

Like IPV, this subject is very real, and can be a difficult subject matter to address because it deals with a person's perception about what violence really is. It is known that a woman who experiences violence and aggression from their mate will leave and go back an average of seven times over the course of their relationship. This number only reflects the number of woman who have reported the issue to either the authorities or an agency who helps battered women. There are MANY women who experience intimate partner violence, sexual, emotional, psychological, and physical abuse daily and NEVER REPORT IT to anyone! If you recall from page 31, domestic violence is something that happens over a period of time. In the beginning, the person is everything you want them to be, but then eventually they start trying to control your thoughts, actions, views and opinions about everything. They also try to isolate you from your friends, family members, and other people all in an attempt to get you to do everything they want you to do. They make themselves your god by telling you they are the only people who will ever love and understand you. Defining your 80/20 is KEY so that you can see these types of behaviors early on in the relationship and take appropriate action to remove yourself from a relationship that is not healthy and ideal. This book is written to help women identify what they need to be happy in an effort to PREVENT domestic violence from occurring in their lives. Once people understand and accept they do not have a right to control others, they can set healthy boundaries and triggers to prevent themselves from being controlled by others as well as from trying to control others.

VIOLENCE IN THE HOME

Women who have children must also recognize their role as the first teachers their children have to defining what is acceptable behavior. Children living in homes where EMOTIONAL, MENTAL, PSYCHOLOGICAL, PHYSICAL, AND CHILD ABUSE occur on a daily basis learn to accept the abuse as normal behavior in their relationships with others. Mothers who demean and disrespect their children verbally are also teaching them to accept that behavior from others. When women establish their home as a SAFE HAVEN for themselves and their children, we will see a SHIFT in how men treat themselves, their families, and others.

It starts at Home
Then it can impact our neighborhoods and communities
Then the city, state, and the nation.

We are out of order in this country, because we are out of order in our homes. We must take back control and order of our homes in a healthy, loving, and responsible way.

BULLYING/STALKING

When someone is being bullied or stalked, they tend to isolate themselves from others, due to their feelings of fear and helplessness, which can cause them to feel sadness, depression, and emotional stress and strain. People who bully or stalk others innately are looking for attention. They have low self-esteem and they feel entitled to receive the attention from the object of their affection.

ARE YOU BULLYING SOMEONE

Bullying is a form of emotional, psychological, and even physical harm to someone cyber stalking or bullying are forms of expressions being displayed to harm someone. If you are bullying someone, then you are trying to control them. Go back and read page 31.

ARE YOU BEING STALKED

Stalking is when someone obsesses over you to the point they harass you and start watching your every move. This is unhealthy behavior and should not be taken lightly or tolerated. Both forms should be reported to the appropriate authority.

COPING AS A TEEN/YOUNG ADULT

The middle/high school years of an individual's life is the period when they are trying to figure out who they are and they desire autonomy and the opportunity to make decisions on their own terms (with adult guidance at times). If a child is being bullied, they won't feel comfortable telling their parents. They try to work it out for themselves. Encourage the teenagers in your life to talk openly about the stressful situations they may be experiencing.

COPING AS A PARENT

The teenage/young adult years are challenging for both parents and individuals, but as a parent, be sure you establish an open, honest, relationship with your young adults where they feel comfortable expressing themselves even if it makes you as an adult uncomfortable. Have monthly family meetings where you encourage all family members to uplift one another, and to share and express their concerns and the issues they are facing on a day to day basis. Let them know they are not alone. Even though it may feel as if they don't hear you, they are. Be involved in their lives and be connected with them by knowing who their friends are and even their friend's parents. Get involved in their world. They may act like they don't want you there, but in reality, they really do!

DEALING WITH UNDESERVED REJECTION FROM OTHERS

When you recognize you are being rejected or that the people in your life are not treating you the way you feel you should be treated, you have to slow down, and try to understand what is causing the rejection with your friend or loved one. When the rejection you are facing in life was NOT directly or indirectly caused by you, that is the time you have to cling to God's word and trust He can help you cope with the emotional and psychological attacks against you. When people reject you, your flesh wants you to lash out against them. Because your flesh is weak, your response to the problem will not be pleasing to God. When other's attack or forsake you, look at it as an opportunity where God might see you are getting too "comfortable" in your current situation and in order for you to prepare for the things He has in store in your future, he might have to make your current environment "uncomfortable" so that you can trust and lean on Him more in that area. When God is trying to tell you something, this type of rejection feels unbearable because you know you did not "cause" or "deserve" it. However, on the other side, it will be for your good and in your favor when you wait on the Lord and trust Him through the process.

Another reason rejection is a Crumzy situation is because people don't have a back up plan in case their first plan doesn't work out the way they want it too. I like to encourage people to have an A, B, and a C plan. If the A plan doesn't work, then try the B plan. If the B plan doesn't work, then go to the C plan. When I lost my job in 2016, I found myself working on a G, H, I, J plan because I had to stay optimistic and press through the financial and emotional toll not obtaining a job was trying to take against my self-esteem. As a believer, I knew God had a plan devised for me, even if I was not able to understand his "infinite" wisdom at that moment. When you find yourself dealing with any form of rejection you have to ask yourself

A) Did you bring this on yourself?

B) Avoid personalizing about the issue (thinking it's your fault or something you caused).

C) Sometimes people reject you because they want you to yearn for them more.

D) Sometimes they reject you because they don't understand you or they can't get you to change.

If you don't deserve the rejection, don't take it personally. It may not be you. It very well may be them and their issue! Stand in your truth even in the midst of the storm or when it feels like it's too hot to handle. The battle is not yours, it's the Lord's. You'll have to be patient and trust in Him more than your flesh.

DEALING WITH REJECTION YOU DESERVED TO RECEIVE

Like undeserved rejection, when you recognize you are being rejected or people in your life are not treating you the way you feel you should be treated, you have to slow down, and take time to reflect on what you did or said that may have caused them to reject you. If they tell you it's because of something you have done, and you don't see it, go back to pages 26 - 31 and review the section for unhealthy communication behaviors. People reject you because they don't feel comfortable telling you they either 1) don't like you personally, 2) they don't like something that you are doing, 3) or it's because of something you have done. In order to fix the issue, complete the following steps

1. Ask them If they would share with you what it was or what it is you are doing or have done that has caused them to treat you differently.
2. Once they tell you what it is, even if you do not believe it to be your truth, it is THEIR TRUTH. Accept what is being said on the merit that in that moment, it is how they feel.
3. Don't feel angry about their reflection, clarify for them their misunderstanding about the situation. Many times the problem is due to a communication or misunderstanding more than it is something you actually did.
4. If what they are saying is the truth, help them to understand your position about it. There will be many times when you won't be able to repair a broken relationship, especially when it causes you to lose sight of who you are or what you need to be happy. Always remember your 80/20. If the issue is repairable, it can go into your 20%, but it should never take away from your 80%.

Not all rejection is bad rejection. There will be people who should not be in your inner circle. Time may heal all wounds. If it does not, then it is not meant for that relationship to be maintained. Appreciate the time you had with them and pray that God continues to cover you, as well as bless them. Also pray for them because if it is not your fault, and if it's God's will, then they will be back.

CRUMZY SITUATIONS

PARENTS WHO WON'T LET GO

One of the greatest joys in the world is to give life to a child and to see them grow into an individual ready to take the world on by storm. But some parents find it difficult to let go and allow their children to make their own decisions. Parents need to be prepared for the different life transitions their child will face so they can be flexible when changes occur.

⇒ **Infants - Six Years of Age.** Parents should know that their child's brain is still developing and even though it seems as if the child is as smart as an adult, because their brain is still developing, they won't remember a lot of things that happen during these years. Parents may get frustrated with their children because it seems as if the child should remember what the parent told them. Be patient understanding they are doing what they are supposed to be doing at that age.

⇒ **Seven - Twelve:** Parents need to teach their children rules, boundaries, work ethic, respect, and appreciation. When children are given too much at an early age, they grow up expecting everything they want to be given to them, thus the term "Entitled." It is important to teach your children these things so they can transition into their teenage years prepared to receive rejection from their peers and have an understanding that it is ok. They also must learn how to respect adults in authority so even though it may be hard to set "strict" boundaries with them, it is for their good.

⇒ **Twelve - Nineteen:** These are the years when teenagers "appear" to be fighting with their parents, family members, peers, and the other adults in their life like their teachers. What they are trying to do is define themselves, and exercise a sense of independence. They want autonomy and the ability to be "trusted" with making decisions. Trust is something that should be earned and if you do not teach them these ethics and tools during their early developmental years (7 - 12), they will struggle during their teenage years. Create a sense of openness and honesty with your teenagers and this will help them transition through these years.

⇒ **Young Adults:** When young adults have not been given a sense of independence and the ability to learn from their mistakes during their teenage years, they appear afraid to try, and thus their parents are afraid to let them fail. Failing and falling is a natural part of experiencing life. Don't be selfish and try to overprotect your young adults. Give them the wings and encouragement to fly and be free knowing you will be there just in case they fall or they need to come home to rest a while.

PARENTS "DEMANDING" RESPECT FROM THEIR ADULT CHILDREN

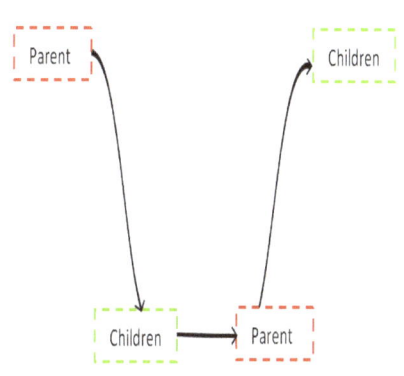

It is difficult for parents to let their grown adult children make their own decisions especially when their parents do not feel it is in their best interest. When teenagers start living their lives as young adults, they desire "autonomy", or the ability to make their own decisions. When children are young, there is an identified level of authority that should exist between parents and their children. But when the children start living their lives as young adults (19-25), and then as adults (26+), especially when they live in their own homes and are paying their own bills, they no longer feel like "children", but they desire to be respected as an adult. Yes, the adults (parents and grandparents) have gotten older, but many parents fight to try to get respect from their adult children because they see their children no longer accept their parent's views and opinions. That difference in opinions is not disrespect, but just a difference of opinions. Parents and especially grandparents find it VERY hard accepting boundaries from their kids and grandchildren. Parents need to let go and accept "BALANCE" and even "BOUNDARIES" by focusing all of their energy on their young adult children. Because when the roles reverse, the children become the adults, and when the new life transition occurs, the parents become **EQUAL** with their adult children. The parents become the children, and then later in life, the adult children have to take care of their parents. If the parents are not willing to let go and respect their children's decisions, when the parents become elderly, they will continue fighting for "respect" with their children which can possibly cause hurt and harm to their relationship. It is not that the children don't respect their parents, they just want their parents to respect them and the great work they have done with their lives. When you see them for who they are, RECEIVE IT.

Parents should also be mindful is their adult children notice how easy it is for you to spoil your grandchildren because they accept you for the person you are to them today. However, don't forget to work just as hard to mend your relationship with your children if it is strained because of the issues that existed during their childhood. They remember the times in the past when you were not able to give them what you are giving your grandchildren. You can't fix the past, but you can redefine your relationship with your adult children going forward! Don't forget they still want to be spoiled too!

IRRESPONSIBLE PARENTS

Although this is not a relationship between a man and a wife, parents are their children's first teachers and we have become a neighborhood, community, society, and nation who expect other people to take care of our children and families. Every child deserves to have the first two levels on Maslow's Hierarchy of Needs met on a daily basis (on page 59). When that child's basic needs are not met, children find themselves at a disadvantage from their friends and peers. Violence between children occur because a child is jealous of what another child has. Society is teaching our children to "believe" they have a right to receive whatever they want, and what others have without giving any consideration or concern if their parents can afford to provide it for them or not. Many times the materialistic thing the child is asking for is not something they need, it is something they want and many parents justify getting it for their child even when they can't afford to do so. Children need boundaries and balance. Their first of many NO's they should receive should come from their parents and not their teacher, their neighbors, their friends, or law enforcement. Children are gifts and should be cherished, loved, respected, and taken care of like a precious gift. They are not meant to be used, mistreated, or leveraged for financial gain. It is not the school district, the community agency, or the government's job to take care of our children. Why are we afraid to hold parents accountable and responsible for the actions of their children? Laws are now created to hold teenagers responsible for the crimes they commit, even though many of them commit the crimes because their basic needs are not being met, and yet, we are not holding their parent's responsible for not taking care of their children's needs through their childhood, and adolescent developmental stages.

Yes I was a statistic. I had my daughter one week after I graduated high school and even though I married her father at 19, he was still my baby daddy because he was not really ready to be a father. I knew that, but like other young single women, I too "loved him" and wanted at least 5 mini me's even though God only gave one in the form of my daughter. I am grateful that he only blessed me with one because I was not financially ready to be a parent of the five I thought I wanted. God gave me what I needed, but for this section, women should slow down and choose WISELY when, with whom, and ensure they are ready to establish a home where everyone's needs are being met without struggling, stress, or additional strain on themselves and others.

DEALING WITH DISRESPECTFUL CHILDREN

Parents are the first and primary teachers of their children. When children are between the ages of 3 - 10, they see their parents and the adults in their family as their first teachers of acceptable communication forms with others. When children are raised in a home where they constantly hear verbal abuse or where the adults in the family curse at one another, shout, yell, or exhibit aggressive behavior, they become teenagers who display verbal and even physical aggression against others. Parents who do not exhibit behavior where they respect and have boundaries with others, teach their children to model that same behavior. It is amazing to see parents who are appalled at their child's behavior but won't look in the mirror at themselves. If you desire to have teenagers who respect others, you must show respect to them at all times. You can't verbally abuse your children, and then expect them to become happy, supportive, appreciative, and respectful teenagers and adults. The same basic needs identified by Abram Maslow (p. 59) apply to children, and when they do not feel their basic needs are met, they too feel unloved, unappreciative, and even not wanted. Be mindful of how you speak to your children, family members, and especially your friends and strangers. Your children are always watching and learning from you. You must strive to model the behavior you want to see in your children. Hurt people, Hurt people. Hurt children grow up to become Hurt people, who Hurt people!

CRUMZY SITUATIONS

DEALING WITH BABY DADDY/MOMMA ISSUES

Women have to stop blaming men or their "BABY'S DADDY" for not stepping up to the plate to take care of "his responsibility." First and foremost, when women have unprotected sex with men, who then find out they're pregnant, and the man tells her he does not want to be a father, he is actually saying HE DOES NOT WANT TO HAVE CHILDREN WITH YOU! This is a hard revelation for women to understand. When a woman decides to have a child by a man that stated he was not ready, or did not want to have her child, she is going to endure 18+ years of heartache, frustration, despair and a CRUMZY situation with him, because he really did not want to be responsible like that in the first place. Because of the nature of the relationship, he may doubt the child is really his because he accepts the fact that she might have other sexual partners. If he is not in a COMMITTED, MONOGAMOUS relationship with you, you are just a side chick, a booty call, or someone he just wants to have sex with. All of these situations will cause you pain when you choose to conceive a baby under these circumstances and thus the term CRUMZY situation.

Ladies, your baby is a blessing, but be prepared to raise the child alone for the next 18+ years without emotional and financial support. In the beginning, he will state emphatically that he does not want to be a father. Just because a man tries to take care of his child, does not mean he wants to be in a relationship with you. Stop trying to make a man who is not ready to be a parent, be a your child's FATHER. There is a difference. Slow down and stop getting yourself into these situations. If a man does not try to be in your child's life, stop asking him too. You shouldn't want someone around your child who won't give them genuine love and support. When he is ready, he'll let you know. If he does not, you do what you need to do to take care of the baby. God will give you everything you need just like He has given all of the other single moms who have raised great wonderful kids who became a blessing to their moms, and the world. God may even send you a true man of God to raise your child, but you have to get yourself prepared for him. Money can't buy love, and the money you will fight him in court to take care of your child will cause a rift and contention between you both. Yes, child support is important, but stop looking for MORE! Stop putting SOLE blame on the him when you allowed yourself to be in that predicament. Take responsibility for your actions and stop playing the VICTIM. Stop believing there are not consequences for your actions. When we do things out of order, we will endure trials and tribulations because of our actions. This does not mean God does not forgive us. Even when we receive His grace and mercy, we will still have to deal with the consequences for our actions. And some of those consequences can last a lifetime.

IF I CAN'T BE THE CAKE, I WON'T BE THE CRUMZ

FAMILY VS RELATIVES

My Godmother told me her definition of family and that freed my life. She said "FAMILY are those who lift you up, support you, embrace you, and appreciate you for being the person that you are. They love you unconditionally. Those other folks who share the same DNA as you do are just RELATIVES". As I also reflected on her words, these two scriptures came to mind:

Proverbs 17:17: A friend loves at all times, and a brother is born for adversity.

Proverbs 3:29: Do not plan evil against your neighbor, who dwells trustingly beside you.

Once I heard her perspective and as I meditated on these scriptures, I changed my views about who I considered family versus relatives. Many times family members hurt one another because of unhealthy learned behaviors. Until you establish healthy boundaries with your family members about your expectations on how you want to be treated, you will accept unhealthy treatment from others because those unhealthy responses feel normal and acceptable behavior to you. When you define your 80/20, you begin setting boundaries with people who do not genuinely appreciate and love you and many times the first group of people to set boundaries with are your immediate and extended family members. If they can't respect the boundaries you are setting, then put them in your RELATIVE category and learn to love them from a distance. Many times your friends will in fact be there for you when your relatives won't, and this is why God wants us to appreciate the strangers He puts in your life who will provide you support, love, and appreciation. They will become your cheerleaders especially when the RELATIVES in your life don't know how to be your cheerleader, or they don't desire to be. A friend will be closer to you than any brother. And I personally have three brothers who I do not have a relationship with but I am grateful to the people God has put in my life who show me genuinely respect, appreciate, and love me. Many times the first set of people you have to be delivered from will be your RELATIVES!

RESPECT VS. DISRESPECT

      Today the definition of respect does not have the same meaning as it did for older generations. Adults born before 1970 see the issues of the world with a "similar" viewpoint, because they were raised with similar morals, values and ethics. Once national and global access to information became available 24 hours a day, 7 days a week through mediums like television, radio, and the Internet, our morals and ethical values began to be influenced by other cultural viewpoints. QUORA defines disrespects as *"When one's behavior offends another to such a degree that 70% of the populace agrees with that viewpoint."* The Silent Generation (those born around 1921) through Generation X (those born through 1965) may feel the same way about disrespectable types of behaviors like:

⇒ Not saying please and thank you.

⇒ When someone enters the room and they don't acknowledge the people there by saying hello.

⇒ If someone borrows money and they take their time paying it back.

⇒ Not respecting someone's age difference or experience - whether they are 16 or 75 people should be respected for who they are.

⇒ Not listening when someone is speaking by interrupting them mid sentence.

⇒ Asking someone to do something with you , then cancelling the plans at the last minute and NOT telling them.

⇒ Showing up late and keeping people waiting.

⇒ Never returning a call or text but you get upset when they do that to you.

⇒ Wearing sagging pants until your undergarments show.

⇒ Children talking back to adults and talking word for word with adults.

⇒ Trying to force your views and opinions on others when they do not agree with you.

⇒ Men not opening the door for women.

      Now, Generation Y, and the younger generation (1966 - those born today) do not feel the same way about the items on this list. When you feel as if you are being "disrespected" by someone, be sure they have the same viewpoint and understanding about the issue that you have because people do not always feel the same way about a behavior. Because you feel strongly about it does not necessarily mean it is COMMON SENSE to others! This is especially true for the older generation's view when they say you are being "DISRESPECTFUL." They don't realize your views about it might not be the same as theirs.

COMMON SENSE IS NOT SO COMMON ANYMORE

Be mindful that your views, opinion, and perception about behaviors may not be the same as your coworkers, friends, family members, and associates. America has become a land of many nationalities, religious views, and different generations. If someone does something that bothers you, don't think of it as disrespectful" or say to yourself they don't have "common sense". Have a conversation with them and create an educational opportunity to share with them that their behavior bothers you. Even if they do not agree with you, you should be comforted knowing that you have shared your boundaries and expectations with them. If they don't agree with you, then that is someone you might need to definitely set "stronger" boundaries while recognizing they are just as entitled to their views and opinions like you. Examples of common types of behavior that aren't so "common" any more are;

⇒ Women wearing skirts that reveals their genital area when they sit down or bend over.
⇒ Women wearing tights and leggings as if they are pants (we can see your underwear).
⇒ Eating in front of others, or entering a room with food and not offering to share what you have with others, or not calling in advance to ask if there is something the might need for you to pick up for them before you arrive.
⇒ Replying to an email and including people who do not need to be informed.
⇒ Want people to remember and acknowledge you on your birthday and holidays, but they don't extend the same courtesy.
⇒ Not cleaning up after yourself especially at someone else's home.
⇒ Changing infants diaper directly on someone's couch. REALLY?
⇒ People wearing their pants so that others can see their underwear.
⇒ Coloring your hair. Be mindful of the "corporate culture" or corporate expectations (what type of job/career do you expect to have).

THE PITFALLS OF ONLINE DATING/CATFISHING

The dynamics of dating, communication, and meeting your soul mate have changed dramatically over the last 10 - 15 years. There are many websites where people post their pictures and a bio about themselves with the hope to attract long, lasting love. However, people who post their profiles can over state and misrepresent themselves. Whether you choose to use an online dating service or go on a blind date with someone recommended by a friend, family member, or coworker, the art of effective communication has not changed and you can't discern if the person you have met online is worthy of your time if you have not established your 80/20 and learned how to look beyond the nice pictures and the words they are telling you.

Don't get caught up and carried away by the words a person tells you until they can back them up with action. Whatever method you use to meet people, the first step in the process is GETTING TO KNOW THEM. Women believe they can tell if a man is marriage material by the words he tells her. Time needs to be spent getting to know a person and that time equates to at least 90 days or more. Don't get trapped into sending them money or paying for their bills, cell phones, and other expenses until you know for a fact they are worthy of your time and you are in a relationship with them. Manipulators use the Internet to prey on people who appear lonely, and who appear to do anything to be in a relationship. Time can reveal whether or not the person you have met online is real and not lying. If they don't ask you to be in a relationship with them, YOU AREN'T. Just because they call you or message/text you, idoes not mean they want to be in a relationship with you. It just means they are trying to get to know you. You can't be cat fished or fooled unless you imagine there is more to the situation than what is really there. Slow down and make them prove their intentions with you through their actions.

DEALING WITH LOVED ONES WITH MENTAL/DRUG ADDICTIONS

It is very hard to watch your loved one deteriorate due to a mental illness and/or drug addiction. They reach out asking for you to give them money, and for you to do things for them at odd and inconvenient times of the day. They fight with the people who want to help them and when they not only have a mental illness, but they may be struggling with alcohol and drug usage, it makes it even more difficult.

SINGLE DIAGNOSIS

Single diagnosis is when your family member is only dealing with one condition like drugs, alcohol, or a mental illness. Many times medication can help them if they are willing to take the meds and get better. Because they don't like how the medication makes them feel, they fight the process of getting better. It also makes it hard just trying to help them. If you can get them to get help earlier in the process, the steps to healing and recovery are much easier.

DUAL DIAGNOSIS

Dual diagnosis is when the person has more than one medical condition such as bipolar schizophrenia and they use drugs. It is difficult to treat a person who has more than one medical condition or vis a versa because the medications that are prescribed to them can have a negative reaction to their drug/alcohol use and many times, individuals who have a mental illness try to use drugs as a remedy. This section was created just as an indicator that loving someone who has multiple medical conditions or who also uses drugs along with their medical conditions can be emotionally, physically and financially challenging. Especially when you feel helpless. Many times, these individuals are categorized as homeless because it is difficult to have them in your home because of their hygienic issues and their tendency to steal from you. My family found a solution by establishing room and board for our family member in a local establishment where he could live independently and we can check in on him and take him food periodically. This is a great solution for us because he is no longer living in the street, or showing up unexpectedly at odd hours of the night looking for us to feed him and give him money. Search for programs, shelters, or community hotels where your family member can live there independently. It will give your family some peace of mind knowing they are sheltered because sometimes other than praying, that is all you might be able to do to help them.

NOT APPRECIATING/DISRESPECTING GOOD MEN

Because women do not know how to recognize "good men" for the bad ones, many men feel women overlook them because they are not AGGRESSIVE or DISRESPECTFUL to them. Women mistakenly believe men who are aggressive are just trying to protect them. A man who lines up with the definition of manhood outlined on pages 60 - 64, are the type of men you should want to be in a healthy relationship with. It is okay to have friends. I tell many women, go to dinner, movies, and socialize with men, without establishing attachments or "labels." Get to know who he is as a man and a person. Aggression is NEVER a healthy sign that someone cares for you. It just means they do not know how to express themselves in a different manner. It also means they grew up in an aggressive home and thus, you will need to define your boundaries, and if they try to cross them, then that is not the person for you. A man after your heart, and a kind, soft-spoken, man who shows you he loves you enough to "hear" your concerns, and he is willing to make adjustments, is not a WEAK man. He is a man to be revered, appreciated, and loved. But only if you are truly ready for a Good Man! Define your 80/20 so you can see him for the great Man of God he really is!

THIS ONE IS FOR THE GOOD DUDES!

LOANING MONEY TO FRIENDS/FAMILY

      The hardest thing about loaning money, is expecting it to be paid when they said they would. The Bible says *"Give freely"* as well as *"Do not Withhold what you owe to others."* Many times as a Christian, you find it difficult to discern if you should loan money to the person asking it of you. If you do not have the money to loan without needing it to be repaid in a timely fashion, then you are not loaning it "freely" and therefore you are not in a position to do so. It is also not wise to loan someone money if it is going to hurt you financially to do so. I have experienced a few situations where the person did not pay me back when they said they would and when I asked them about it, they asked me if I was trying to "clock their paycheck" or they said "why you be all in my pockets?" Sometimes you are not rewarded for your kindness, so you have to put up boundaries to protect yourself and your heart which are referred to as "your feelings, and your emotions". If I don't have it to give without stressing out when it will be repaid, I don't give it. The love of money is the root to all evil and can break up relationships. Sometimes tough love, is the best love but also pray and search within your heart asking the Lord to reveal if you are in a position to loan money to the person.

Psalms 37:25-26: *"I have been young and now I am old, Yet I have not seen the righteous forsaken Or his descendants begging bread. All day long he is gracious and lends, And **his descendants are a blessing**."*

Deuteronomy 15:11: *"For the poor will never cease to be in the land; therefore I command you, saying, 'You shall **freely** open your hand to your brother, to your needy and poor in your land."*

Proverbs 3:27-28: *"**Do not withhold good from those to whom it is due,** When it is in your power to do it. Do not say to your neighbor, "Go, and come back, And tomorrow I will give it," When you have it with you."*

Matthew 5:42: *"Give to him who asks of you, and do not turn away from him who wants to borrow from you."*

GENERATIONAL "HABITS" NOT "CURSES"

     The life patterns and cues we learn as children in relationships with our family members, relatives, and close friends become the life habits we form with others. Whereas there may be generational curses, unhealthy communication styles are not curses, but they are normalized habits. Until you learn different tools and techniques on responding to others in a healthy manner, you will inadvertently teach your children how to disrespect others, and how to be disrespected by others.

     Changing your habits will help you change the way your family members relate to one another. It starts with you having a made up mind, and heart to be the difference you want to see if your life and within your family!

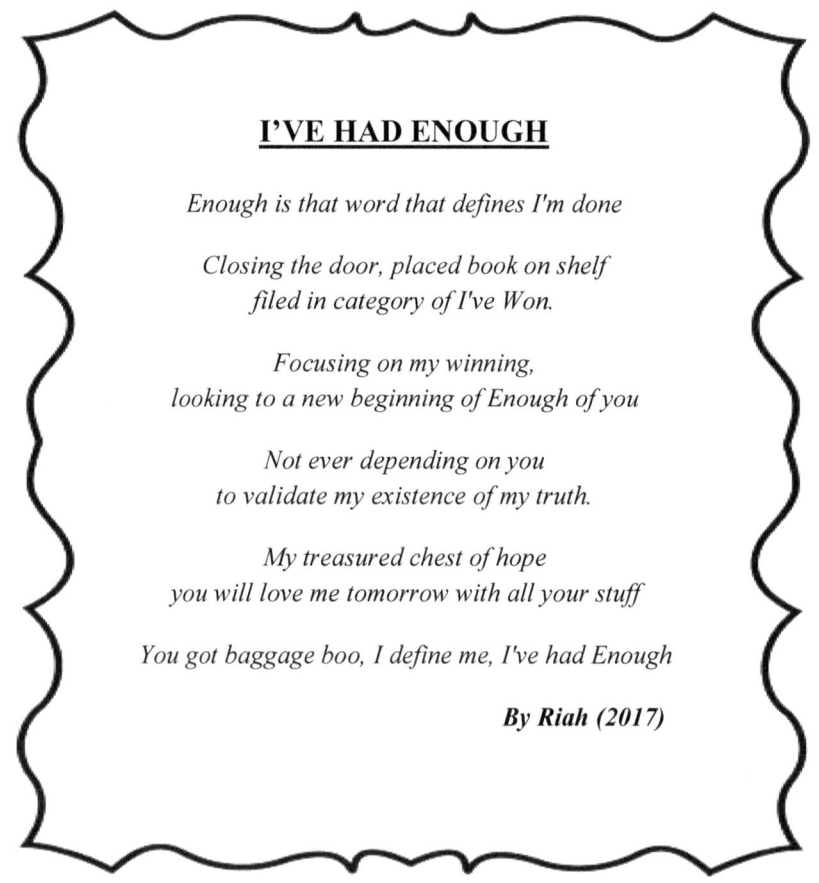

I'VE HAD ENOUGH

Enough is that word that defines I'm done

*Closing the door, placed book on shelf
filed in category of I've Won.*

*Focusing on my winning,
looking to a new beginning of Enough of you*

*Not ever depending on you
to validate my existence of my truth.*

*My treasured chest of hope
you will love me tomorrow with all your stuff*

You got baggage boo, I define me, I've had Enough

By Riah (2017)

NOT KNOWING YOU MATTER!

When you grow up in a household where you are taught to take care of everyone but yourself, you become an adult who does not know how to take care of yourself or know how to take time out for yourself. You feel appreciated when you do for others and you are uncomfortable when others try to do for you. This is a life learned habit that will take you some time to find your voice, and your joy so that you can start loving yourself without the need for affirmation from others. Until you realize YOU MATTER, you will always seek affirmation and attention from others, and when they speak negatively about you; their opinions can cause you great emotional pain.

DEALING WITH USERS/MANIPULATORS

A person who loves someone who is a user and a manipulator is in love with the idea of "helping them", "changing them", or "supporting their dreams and ideas". Unfortunately, users and manipulators do not care if you have your own dreams or ideas. Users and manipulators will always try to guilt you into feeling that they are always right, and you are wrong. They make you feel as if you owe them something, and that you must do what they tell you to do. Users and manipulators will never let you feel appreciated, understood, and loved because their whole focus is getting what they want at any cost regardless of the people it may hurt. They only think of themselves and what they want. Nothing else and no one else matters. It actually is not a good idea for you to have them in your life because their energy and resources cause you to feel that your spending your time on your dreams and ideas will take you away from focusing on them! Never lose sight of your 80/20 and stop trying to rescue and fix them.

The first step in loving yourself and recognizing you matter is to identify your 80/20. What are the things that make your heart sing, cause you pain, and that get on your nerve. You are uniquely and wonderfully made and until you find the power of self love, you can't find your self-esteem, self-worth, self-identify, and even your self-respect; you won't believe you matter, like God says you do. Start here and now by doing what is needed to embrace that concept and begin the process of loving yourself and defining your 80/20.

NOT BEING PREPARED FOR LIFE TRANSITIONS

Each of us will experience the different transitions in life, and yet nine times out of ten we are not prepared for them when they occur. When you are not prepared for unexpected changes in your life, you find yourself uncomfortable and the emotions and feelings you experience when you are uncomfortable cause you to innately project those unhealthy emotions on others. Be prepared for the different life transitions outlined below, and define your plan for them. It's better safe than sorry, and if you have a plan, then you are one step closer to being prepared and not caught off guard.

- ⇒ Different stages of life
    - ⇒ Infants (birth to 1) Protect their fragile bodies.
    - ⇒ Toddler (2 - 5) Prepare for temper tantrums they won't remember having when they get older.
    - ⇒ Pre-Teen (6 - 12) Teaching them respect, work ethics and healthy communication skills.
    - ⇒ Teenager (13 - 19) preparing for their need to "define" themselves and establish their own space and individuality.
    - ⇒ Young Adult (20 - 35) Preparing them to handle responsibilities and living on their own.
    - ⇒ Middle Age (36 - 40) Preparing for physical and health changes. You're not as young as you think you are.
    - ⇒ Aging (40+) Preparing to see your parents and grandparents age and need you to take care of them while at the same time, you're finally positioned to take care of yourself.
- ⇒ Grandparents and their Grandchildren - Sometimes grandparents get to fix the relationship and parenting issues they had with their children on their grandchildren. Just understand that the adult kids may feel a little "Crumzy" about that because they did not receive all of the love and attention that is being showered on the grandchildren. The parents don't mean to be jealous, but they are humans and it's never too late going forward to rebuild and redefine a new relationship with your children. Yes it will take work, but it should be worth it.
- ⇒ Health changes - As you get older, your body changes along with your health.
- ⇒ Financial disparities - Not having a financial back up plan can cause you to become depressed when you can't afford the things you want and need. Make sure you know your credit history, your credit score, and interest rates you are being charged for products and services you receive. Be credit conscious and savvy.
- ⇒ Death in family/loved one - There is nothing that can prepare you for the heartache of missing the presence of your loved one that's no longer here. However, having a healthy conversation about such losses and creating a support system of family, relatives, and friends can help you get through the emotionally trying days and especially the holidays that remind you they are no longer there with you.

TRUTH VS LIES

When a person says something that you feel is a lie, you have to learn how to separate your feelings and emotions from how you handle the situation. First, if the information they have shared is not YOUR TRUTH, it can very well be "their truth" or "their perception" about the issue. When you recognize someone is not hearing you, or does not understand your views or position about the matter, then you have to learn how to "agree to disagree" by

1) Acknowledging that you heard and understand their views, recognizing you do not agree with it.

2) Restate your position "differently" to see if they will understand what you are saying if it is said in a different way.

3) If they do not understand your truth, then you will have to agree to disagree and table the discussion for a different day.

Many people want to force you to accept their views about an issue that you do not see eye to eye with them on. No one has a right to make you accept something that is not your truth. That is called manipulation. Many times, people will get upset, tell you they are hurt all with the goal of getting you to accept their truth as your own. You can always be swayed to accept a LIE as the TRUTH when you do not know what you really feel about the issue. Define your 80/20. The key to recognizing how to accept the difference in views cannot happen if you have not searched within yourself to define who you are. Learn how to stop going along to get along. In the end, it only prolongs the inevitable which is you're standing on what is in your best interest when you disagree with someone. Pray for them and for clarification to understand the difference in your viewpoint. It might seem like you won't hear from the Lord if your heart is troubled, weary, or saddened. Don't' receive not understanding a different viewpoint as your failure. If you trust and believe He is there with you, when you receive guidance from the Holy Spirit, you will find the clarity you need to state your case, as well as an opportunity to seek the Lord's will and understanding about how you should handle the situation asking Him what you can do to fix the issue, or helping you to set strong boundaries because of the differences.

RELATIONSHIPS WITH PEOPLE INCARCERATED

Women in a relationship with a man on parole or probation must review Maslows' chart on page 59 which can help them evaluate if the person is emotionally and psychologically capable of loving you. Someone in need of shelter, clothing, money, and security is not able to give and receive love from you until those needs are met. This is why many women spend all of their financial resources trying to help a man get to level 3 where he is capable of loving someone other than himself. Because of a woman's innate need to care for and nurture others, she will recognize his need for help and a person incarcerated will use that against her. A "healthy" man will do the work that is needed to prevent this situation from happening. Men in jail have nothing else to do other than prey upon women who will take care of them. A real man will take care of himself and his responsibilities. A man who expects a woman to put money on his commissary, accept all of his telephone calls, send food, clothing, cigarettes, and take money from her home to take care of him is no man at all. He is a USER and a MANIPULATOR. Especially when he has many women he reaches out to do all of these things for him. He will use his mother, sister, children, other family members, and especially have a harem of other women to give him the things he feels he wants because he is in no position to get them for himself. Women have to understand they are not only taking money away from themselves, but they are robbing their children by using the money that is needed for them on her incarcerated lover. Spending weekends in jail and taking your children to see your "boyfriend" or even their "father" is not a healthy experience for them. Your husband or boyfriend did the crime, so they have to do the time. It is emotionally draining to see an incarcerated man get out of jail, and then get thrown back in there for doing the same thing or something else just as stupid and irresponsible. Women who date or maintain relationships with men in jail are women who get emotional satisfaction from "rescuing" someone. For some women, they like "believing" they are in control of the situation and they feel empowered helping him. A man incarcerated will tell you everything you need to hear, to get you to believe you are his everything; because he needs you to continue spending your money on him. Be sure to evaluate if your needs are getting met (your 80%) from this 20% situation. Stop putting someone else's needs before yours especially when they are in no position to do the same.

LOVE VS LUST

Many people have heard the saying "Too Much Of Anything Is A Sin." What you must understand about the wisdom outlined in the Scriptures is that anytime you indulge in something that either makes you lose control of yourself, or causes you to forsake God and his commandments will inevitably cause you to do things you will regret. When it comes to relationships, the same holds true about sex so the question you should ask yourself is "Are you in Love or in Lust?" When a man does not have much else to give to you, he will master the art of pleasuring a woman because women internalize sex as "love", and they think sex is a pre-requisite or requirement to receiving love from a man. However to a man, sex is just sex. Women need to learn how to separate the difference between the two. When you allow sex and the pleasures of the flesh to control your desires and your relationships, you will always experience heartache and despair. Sex alone is not love. In your 80/20 definition, sex is not the only thing you will list. It usually includes intimacy, romance, communication, and many other needs. The scriptures in the Bible clearly outline God's position about sex, impurity, debauchery, lewdness, and fornication.

REFLECTION SCRIPTURES ABOUT LUST

BOOK	SCRIPTURE
2 Corinthians 12:21	Not repenting one's sexual sins
Galatians 5:19	Acts of the flesh
Hebrews 13:4	Marriage bed kept pure
1 Corinthians 6:9	Sexually immoral nor idolaters will not inherit the kingdom
Matthews 5:28	Lusting is a sin
1 Thessalonians 4:3-5	Controlling your own body
1 Corinthians 6:13-20	Sexual immorality
Mark 7:22-23	Lewdness defiles a person

REFLECTION SCRIPTURES

BOOK	SCRIPTURE
James 1:2-4	When trouble comes in waves after waves
1 Colossians 6:18-20	When you are tempted to commit sexual sins
Mathew 4:1-11	Then you are tempted to do wrong
Act 27:13-26	When you face physical danger
Psalm 37:1-4	When you are bored
Psalm 27	When you are afraid
Psalm 13	When you are lonely
Psalm 107	When you are anxious for those you know
1 John 1:9	When you sin
Psalm 51	When you need forgiveness
Peter 28:13	When you are feeling shame
Hebrews 4:14-16	When you feel no one understands
Peter 11:25	When you are tempted to be stingy
Romans 12:19	When you want to take revenge
Hebrew 13:5	When you feel abandoned
Psalm 46	When you need more than human help
Colossians 1:21-22	When your past haunts you
Psalm 119:9-11	When you need to know how to stay on the right path
Romans 13:12-13	Conducting oneself appropriately
Ephesians 5;15-18	Stop living foolishly

Crumzy situations

THINGS TO KEEP DOING

_____
_____
_____
_____
_____
_____
_____
_____

THINGS TO START DOING

_____
_____
_____
_____
_____
_____
_____
_____

THINGS TO STOP DOING

_____
_____
_____
_____
_____
_____
_____
_____

IF I CAN'T BE THE CAKE, I WON'T BE THE CRUMZ

CRUMZY SITUATIONS

MY 80/20 CRUMZY SITUATION CHECKLIST

- [ ] I WILL define boundaries to keep people from hurting me
- [ ] I WILL define my definition of love
- [ ] I will take responsibilities for how I treat others
- [ ] I not settle for less than being respected, loved, and appreciated
- [ ] I will redefine my definition of FAMILY

OTHER NOTES

_____
_____
_____
_____
_____
_____
_____
_____
_____
_____
_____
_____
_____
_____
_____
_____
_____

IF I CAN'T BE THE CAKE, I WON'T BE THE CRUMZ

CRUMZ SNATCHER
SIDE CHICK/OTHER WOMAN/MISTRESS

At the end of the day, the side chick, THOT, LOOP, and any other slang word or phrase to describe the other woman who is really Ms. RIGHT NOW and not MRS. RIGHT. Women who are willing to be the side chick need to understand they are giving him EXACTLY what he want. He's married or in a relationship with someone else, and you are just for FUN. When a man decides to be in a "RELATIONSHIP" with a woman, he does so because there's something about her that makes him want to be there. Especially when he marries her! If he's not married to her, he is either thinking about marrying her, has kids with her, or she's offering him the basic needs he's struggling to get on his own like shelter and food. In order for him to give all of that up, the OTHER WOMAN has to match or beat what he has at home and nine times out of ten she doesn't. If he only see's her for sex, then that is ALL he wants from her. Most women who have ever been a CRUMZ snatcher eventually realized that other than money, great conversation, and/or sex, that was all she ever got out of it. And, it never lasted long. CRUMZ were not meant to fill you. They leave you hungry for more. If this is your situation, you might as well start over as a CAKE POP and identify your 80/20 so you can stop settling for just CRUMZ! Just because they taste good, doesn't mean the CRUMZ are fulfilling.

BOOK	SCRIPTURE
1 Corinthians 6:19-20	Your body is a temple
2 Peter 1:5-6	Maintaining self control—1
Proverbs 25:26-29	Maintaining self control - 2
Galatians 5:19-26	Flesh vs the Holy Spirit
Romans 8:3-9	Living selfishly with weak boundaries - 1
Galatians 5:16-17	Living selfishly with weak boundaries - 2
Galatians 6:8-9	Living selfishly with weak boundaries - 2
Romans 13:12-13	Let sex, drugs and alcohol control you
Luke 12:14-15	Living for greed
Philippians 3:7-8	Chasing monetary/materialistic things
Proverbs 7:1-27	You are promiscuous

IF I CAN'T BE THE CAKE, I WON'T BE THE CRUMZ

REFLECTIONS FROM CLIENTS

Start loving yourself more and have more self worth

♡

Realizing self worth and understating your value. You MATTER!

♡

Start valuing their time and themselves

♡

Start respecting yourself

♡

Find your own man

♡

Start being the only not and not #2

♡

Start finding yourself as a woman who believes you are worth much more

♡

Start Living

♡

Start finding your own man

♡

Start having more respect for yourself & know your worth

♡

Empowering others, not everything is a competition

♡

Start knowing MY TRUE WORTH!

IF I CAN'T BE THE CAKE, I WON'T BE THE CRUMZ

REFLECTIONS FROM CLIENTS

Stop using excuses

♡

Stop repeating the same behavior

♡

Start respecting yourself

♡

Stop settling and neglecting yourself

♡

*Stop feeling that they are the MANIPULATORS
when they are actually being MANIPULATED*

♡

Stop being disconnected with SELF

♡

*Stop settling and believing the lie that you don't deserve better
Or that there isn't better*

♡

*Stop being heartless and consider the other woman.
What if it was you?*

♡

Stop the craziness in your life

♡

Stop allowing others to define you!

REFLECTIONS FROM CLIENTS

Stop believing someone can't crumb snatch you!

♡

Change the way of communicating when it comes to men

♡

Stop taking what does not belong to you

♡

Stop looking for love in all the wrong places

♡

Stop believing someone can't Crumz Snatch You!

♡

Stop settling for CRUMZ

♡

Stop touching what don't belong to you

♡

Stop allowing people, men and women to take advantage of me!

♡

STOP GIRL. JUST STOP!

CRUMZ SNATCHER - SIDE CHICK

MY 80/20 CRUMZY SITUATION CHECKLIST

- ☐ I recognize that I am settling for less than I deserve
- ☐ I will start over as a Cake Pop and define my 80/20
- ☐ I recognize the harm I am doing to myself and to others
- ☐ I will not be SELFISH and SELF-CENTERED any longer
- ☐ I cannot change the past, but I can start over today going forward

THINGS TO START DOING

_____
_____
_____
_____
_____
_____
_____
_____
_____
_____
_____
_____
_____
_____
_____
_____
_____
_____
_____

IF I CAN'T BE THE CAKE, I WON'T BE THE CRUMZ

CRUMZ SNATCHER - SIDE CHICK

THINGS TO STOP DOING

IF I CAN'T BE THE CAKE, I WON'T BE THE CRUMZ

I DESERVE BETTER

Am I the one you showcase at night
Living a life with you, but constantly hidden out of sight.

Weekends, holidays, family reunions I don't get to do
Back door entrance at my house is what you do, Boo.

I cried last night from all the loneliness I felt in the air
Knowing you only have a couple hours to share.

Then while I wait,
here comes the call,
and you say you can't come
She sick, no babysitter for the kids, and you gotta stay home.

Why, do I keep screaming,
"you gotta get a grip stop thinking so less of yourself"
Tired of being the other whatever I am
and what you want me to be.

I am beat down, torn up from all the passion marks I've embraced
My reflection in the mirror of guilt,
pain and sorrow is the makeup on my face.

People talking, friends laughing, lying, and family calling me names
All on the back of our shared lies, deception,
and lust I want no longer to live in shame.

I deserve better than this, from this trap I will be set free
No More Crumz for me
For I will fly high in the sky like the woman I was created to be.

Bu Riah (2017)

SUMMARY

Establishing a healthy, loving, Godly relationship is not IMPOSSIBLE, but it does take work, and it is something that must be done EVERYDAY, ALL DAY. The work does not end when you're married (Mrs. Cake), because you have to work harder when you are married than when you are single (a Cake Pop) or dating (a Cupcake).

Cake Chronicles was inspired because of the wisdom I discovered in the life lessons my grandmother chose to tell me through her jokes and old sayings. I didn't listen to her at first or try to get an understanding when she started telling them to me. Like most young adults, I too believed the elders in my life couldn't understand or relate to present day circumstances, so I was trying to figure it out on my own. When I got tired of falling, and failing, I remembered the wisdom of my grandmother's sayings and how they actually made sense when I took the time to meditate, and reflect on their true meaning. If I Can't Be The Cake, I Won't Be The Crumz is a metaphor to help women realize they are worth more than the "Crumz" they may be settling for from others. Many times you settle for less than you desire because you haven't been told how to define exactly what would make you happy. Until you understand the meaning of Self-Esteem, Self-Worth, Self Confidence, and Self Love, you will struggle to find true happiness because you are looking for someone else to help you define it. Slow down, and define your 80%. Set healthy, loving, boundaries and never settle for less than the 80% because you will start feeling CRUMZY. Just like a great cake made from scratch, when it comes to defining what you need to be happy, you will need to determine what ingredients or characteristics you need in your relationship with others. You might have to minimize some things, in order to balance out others, or you might need to remove some ingredients and replace them with others because they don't work for you, but overall, like any great cake once it's done right, you will want to continue experiencing more of it.

If I Can't Be The Cake, I Won't Be The Crumz is my Christian Parable, my earthly story with a Heavenly message. Let your light shine so that others can see Christ manifesting in your life. Choose the right ingredients in your Christian character so that others will be drawn to the Christ within you. It is my prayer that the words I have been inspired to write in this book, encourage and motivate you to choose God over the world. Choose Heaven on earth over all the fleshly desires you might be tempted to experience. When you slow down, pray, and ask God to inspire you to live your life according to His will, and His way. The Holy Spirit will order your path and the Lord will put a hedge of protection around you and your descendants. Your life is not your own. May my Grandmother's wisdom and her parables be a blessing to you like they have been a blessing to me, and may you touch and inspire someone like Christ has inspired each of us to do. Find your calling, and that includes keeping healthy loving people close and in your inner circle.

WE ARE THE WOMEN

We are the women,
yes that woman who will celebrate her life
Chosen by God to be friend,
mother, daughter and to some a wife.

We will embrace our many challenges and circumstances,
and soar through the words on the pages
Strolling down our red carpet experience,
heads up strutting our stride through life many stages.

Making many accomplishments one after another,
climbing high mountains, as we go
Conquering fears, achieving our goals
of being a woman embodied in her radiant glow.

We are those women
when that is this and this is that
We take our stance, look life in the eye,
with our tailored suits, pumps, pearls
and our favorite hat.

Preparing an inheritance
of strength for our children,
and a legacy left behind.
When they open the Book of Life
they will see We Are The Women, they will find.

We will wear our Womanhood
and celebrate another sister
while she shares her truth to us.
Celebrating our sisterhood.
Woman to Woman
real Women we grow to trust.

By Riah (2017)

WHEN YOU'VE DONE ALL YOU CAN

When you've done all you can,
STAND

When you've done all you can
PRAY

When you've done all can
ANALYZE

When you've done all you can
SEARCH FOR REVELATION

When you've done all you can
PRAY AGAIN

When you've done all you can
SEARCH FOR CLARIFICATION

And after you've done all you can
LET GOD DO WHAT HE DOES BEST
WORK IT OUT IN YOUR FAVOR!

Mrs. Debbie Cakes

REFERENCES

1. Adam & Eve. Taken from http://www.godandscience.org/images/adam_and_eve.jpg

2. 80/20. Taken from https://8020365.com/wp-content/uploads/2014/11/8020pyramid2.png

3. It's Complicated. Taken from http://cdn.hercampus.com/s3fs-public/2015/01/30/socialmedia-relationships2.jpg

4. What is Dysfunction - https://en.wikipedia.org/wiki/Dysfunctional_family

5. Breaking Free from the Victim Trap. Taken from https://images-na.ssl-images-amazon.com/images/I/517er9V1%2B0L._SX330_BO1,204,203,200_.jpg

6. Self-Esteem and Getting Ahead. Taken from https://www.abebooks.com/9780538705721/Self-Esteem-Ahead-South-Westerns-Life-Series-0538705728/plp

7. Frog in a Pot. Taken from http://draletta.typepad.com/.a/6a00d83527e90e69e2012875fcb34c970c-320pi

8. Ball of emotions - https://sites.google.com/a/simfoods.com/chaplain-services/_/rsrc/1430226637406/inspiration/Tangled%20Ball%20of%20Grief.png

9. Power and Control. Taken from http://www.lfcc.on.ca/power_and_control.jpg

10. The Love Dare. Taken from http://d.christianpost.com/full/62852/img.jpg

11. Codependent No More. Taken from https://images-na.ssl-images-amazon.com/images/I/81UoZA%2BzLXL._AC_UL320_SR216,320_.jpg

12. Imperfect Phrases. Taken from http://www.barnesandnoble.com/p/imperfect-phrases-for-relationships-robert-bacal/1114254390/2686018193835?st=PLA&sid=BNB_DRS_Marketplace+Shopping+greatbookprices_00000000&2sid=Google_&sourceId=PLGoP24104

13. Crazymakers. Taken from http://emp.byui.edu/BEANB/Crazymakers.pdf

14. Love Languages. Taken from http://urbanbushbabes.com/wp-content/uploads/2013/03/Blend500.jpg

15. The Complete Husband. Taken from https://images-na.ssl-images-amazon.com/images/I/51DD8823XJL._SY344_BO1,204,203,200_.jpg

16. Maslow Hierarchy of Needs. Taken from http://timvandevall.com/wp-content/uploads/2013/11/Maslows-Hierarchy-of-Needs.jpg

17. Men are from Mars, Women are from Venus. Taken from https://jameskennedymonash.files.wordpress.com/2013/02/men-are-from-mars-women-are-from-venus-1.jpg

18. Being the Woman God Wants Me to Be. Taken from https://s-media-cache-ak0.pinimg.com/736x/17/31/a4/1731a4bdd69a710a6ce15f2a6bab55c0.jpg

19. Domestic Violence statistics. Taken from http://www.huffingtonpost.com/2014/10/23/domestic-violence-statistics_n_5959776.html

20. Disrespect vs. Respect. Taken from QUORA https://www.quora.com/What-are-some-examples-of-disrespectful-behavior

21. Friends: Taken from https://www.gotquestions.org/friend-stick-closer-brother.html

22. http://www.lulu.com/shop/l-r-highsmith/ascension-into-love/ebook/product-17433896.html

23. Poems by Deborah Hambrick-Elsby published author of "Who Called You?", Arthur House

www.ingramcontent.com/pod-product-compliance
Lightning Source LLC
Chambersburg PA
CBHW040456240426
43665CB00037B/11